Contents

How to use this book

The aim of this book is to give you the means of developing your understanding both of F. Scott Fitzgerald's novel *The Great Gatsby*, and of the issues which you need to address in order to successfully answer examination questions on the novel. It provides an insight into the world of the novel and into the individual vision of Fitzgerald's portrayal of it. It highlights the development of some of the characters and the performance of others true to their type, the major events through which they work out their destinies, and the themes of life and love and human purpose which their interactions raise.

The bold headings highlight key points in the novel's development. Together they summarise the storyline and signpost the development of the characters.

The text summarises the key events and the settings in which they are worked out, and raises elements in the characters' development and the evolution of the themes.

Under the heading **Note** are listed significant aspects which you should not overlook in your analysis, including key aspects in the characters' thinking and behaviour. These entries also highlight the complexities upon which Fitzgerald's individual world vision is founded.

The points listed under the heading **Consider** raise specific matters which you should analyse critically. They require some deep thinking.

The **Select a Quote** entries, identified by ⟨Q⟩ draw your attention to important passages from which you can choose key quotations to support your own analysis of the text. They will provide a useful framework and supporting evidence for examination answers.

Under the heading **Examining the Issues** is a range of test topics. These promote further thinking about the issues and highlight the kinds of exam and discussion questions which could be derived from the part of the text to which they refer.

Examination and Essay Questions are provided as a final chapter. They represent a sample of the popular types of exam questions. The checklists provide you with a start in framing your answer. They identify the matters which you should at least consider in any discussion of the issues which the questions raise.

The page numbers in brackets refer to the Penguin 1990 edition; for those using other editions, sufficient words are given to identify the quotations.

The Great Gatsby

FRANCES RUSSELL MATTHEWS

PHOENIX
EDUCATION

First published in Australia in 1998

Phoenix Education Pty Ltd
PO Box 197, Albert Park 3206
Tel: (03) 9699 8377 Fax: (03) 9699 9242
PO Box 3141, Putney 2112
Tel: (02) 9809 3579 Fax: (02) 9808 1430

ISBN 1 875695 81 8

Edited by Janet Mackenzie
Text design and page make-up by Graphic Divine
Cover design by Sharon Carr
Printed in Australia by Shannon Books

1

F. Scott Fitzgerald and his world

The author

F. Scott Fitzgerald was born just before the end of the nineteenth century, 1896, in St Paul, Minnesota, in the Mid-West of the United States. From 1917 to 1918, he served in the American army in World War I. He published his first novel, *This Side of Paradise*, two years later, and soon after married Zelda Sayre. His novel met with immediate success and launched Fitzgerald and his wife into the glitzy world of the wealthy in the 1920s—the Jazz Age.

The life the couple led embodied all the carelessness, luxury and self-indulgence of the time, as well as the recklessness that grew in the new America which was created out of the ashes and the demoralisation of World War I.

The Great Gatsby, which was published in the middle of the 1920s, captured this new, if degenerate, spirit which submerged America's old-fashioned conservative values. This novel also contains, somewhat ironically, the sense of hopelessness and the lack of a sound foundation that lay behind the party-going of this new world. These values—or lack of values—led finally to the collapse of the lightheartedness of the age and foreshadowed the despair of the Great Depression which dominated the 1930s. They also contributed to the difficulties which permeated Fitzgerald's personal life from the end of the decade.

By the time of his sudden death in 1940, Fitzgerald had written five novels (*This Side of Paradise, The Great Gatsby, The Beautiful and the Damned, Tender Is the Night,* and *The Last Tycoon*), six volumes of short stories, and a selection of autobiographical pieces perhaps aptly named *The Crack-Up*.

The historical and social background

The novel explores a year in the life of America at the beginning of the decade which was to culminate in the greatest economic depression that the world had known. It was a watershed in history—ruled by a riotous, unthinking, selfish escapism (for those who could afford it) from the horrors of the Great War of 1914–18, which had taught Americans, and all participants, that values, belief and life were not forever.

The 1920s was a period of expansion, driven by a social creed of upward mobility. In that decade, America was a mecca for those seeking their fortunes and those who were in search of novelty and entertainment. America was a country quickly becoming confident in its own norms. Its elite had their own music—jazz. (Jazz became more broadly popular during the 1930s.)

The decade was marked by a central irony. Having agreed to prohibition of alcohol, people began partying in grand style. It was the time to be alive, to be young and to be American. The decade even saw the invention of the dry martini.

The economy was booming. President Warren Harding's administration was strong; it was yet to be undermined by the corruption of its senior officials and public demonstration of the selling of government favours. These scandals tainted 1923 and the years following, to culminate at the end of the decade with the literary depiction of the President as a libertine and a slob. It was symptomatic of the times, however, that Harding's successor in August 1923 was a boy from a farm in rustic Vermont, President Calvin Coolidge. The America of his administration experienced the longest housing boom ever recorded and its people the widest distribution of prosperity.

Fitzgerald called the decade the 'greatest, gaudiest spree in history'. Every aspect of American culture was marked by spectacular advances: tens of millions of ordinary families were at last able to gain economic security with access to housing, automobiles, education, and investment opportunities. American literature flourished; so did musical theatre.

American society gained a new cultural awareness, a sensitivity to the value of Americanness and to the importance of its past. America was a community that was growing up. By 1927 the American people saw themselves as creating a new social structure based upon the revolutionary changes brought about by modern methods of production.

Prohibition and the rise of American crime

In December 1917, Congress submitted to the states the Eighteenth Amendment which, when ratified in 1919, changed the American Constitution to ban 'the manufacture, sale or transportation of intoxicating liquors'. The Volstead Act, making America dry, had already been passed. It was now constitutional.

The imposition of Prohibition grew out of a belief that people can create Utopia in the present: that, on American soil, the millennium could be secured in this world as well as in the next. The idealism inherent in the Volstead Act came face to face with another tenet of American society—the importance of unrestricted freedom of enterprise.

The effect of the Volstead Act was to transfer the manufacture, sale and distribution of liquor from legitimate to criminal forces. In the space of a few months, liquor gangsters rose to become more powerful than the judicial system and its enforcers.

Corrupt officials and crime bosses in America's cities made previously unbelievable fortunes out of the liquor trade, instigating sophisticated systems of official bribery and distribution as the basis of their new careers. Territories were carved up and jealously guarded. Any man or woman who wanted to drink alcohol in America could do so. In 1930 Washington DC, for example, had more than twice as many liquor outlets as it had had before Prohibition. Its 700 or so speakeasies were supplied by more than 4000 bootleggers. Arrests for drunkenness trebled during the 1920s.

Prohibition generated enormous funds, which were reinvested in other criminal activities such as prostitution, gambling and drug-smuggling. It ensured that crime in America would forever after be organised on a large scale, and it created distribution and criminal communication networks which still operate today. Its damage to American society was permanent.

The America of the novel

The America of *The Great Gatsby* is not an egalitarian or homogeneous society. It is a world divided on wealth-based class, on geographical bases, on moral values. It is a New World in the process of evolution after the horrors of World War I and still bearing its scars. The East is the setting for America's reinvention of itself. The West, the traditional frontier, has been abandoned to its small-town mentality. The selfish morality of consumerism is the country's new moral code, and the pursuit of wealth and pleasure its new religion.

The America of the novel is characterised by:
- suspicion and isolation of outsiders
- the arrogance of an Establishment founded on Old Money
- the evolution of the New Woman
- social mobility based on wealth
- the emergence of Broadway as a social force
- widespread criminality
- social and personal disintegration
- the alienation of the poor
- islands of wealth surrounded by regions of poverty and despair
- the restlessness and carelessness of the very rich
- violence and death
- the rising influence of technology—business deals over the telephone, the growing dominance of the automobile
- the corruption of the American Dream
- the corruption of love
- the rising power of innuendo and gossip; increasing power of the tabloid newspapers
- adultery and illicit liaisons
- the celebration of youth and its quick corruption
- disintegration
- moments of rare beauty
- a guilty consciousness of the past
- a sense of emptiness, of a yawning abyss behind the glitzy facade
- a desperate clinging to the belief that America is a brave new world, a fertile environment for the realisation of individual dreams.

A step-by-step plan for success in exams

Exam success depends upon your development of an effective plan of attack. The major elements of such a plan are set out in the steps below.

Step 1: Know the novel

Prepare yourself as effectively as you can. This means actually reading the novel closely so that you understand the development of the characters and the evolution of the themes. This close reading in F. Scott Fitzgerald's work is very demanding. You will have to pay attention to nuances of conversation, to brief exchanges between the characters, to their confessions to themselves and to others. You will also need to be alive to class divisions in their world, not only between the rich and the poor but between the Establishment and the *nouveau riche*, that is, between those with old money and those who have newly acquired it. Notice the portrayal of the lives of the poor who live outside the sheltered world of the rich, the bohemian world of Broadway, and the criminal underworld. You will need to be attentive, also, to the movement of the characters between these worlds, and the price that some (Myrtle Wilson, Nick Carraway and Jay Gatsby himself) pay for doing so.

You understand a Fitzgerald novel only when you have got into the minds of the characters, enabling you to nominate the events which show them acting truly to their type, or which demonstrate (even if subtly) how they have matured and revised their opinions of others and of their role in their world. You also need to identify the degree of control that they have over their own lives (and self-image) and over the lives of those around them. In all the novels you will be challenged by a complex chronological and narrative structure. Make sure that you understand the narrator first. After all, it is through his eyes that the rest of the novel's world is interpreted.

Note the lyrical structure of all the novels. Develop a particular sensitivity to Fitzgerald's love of set-pieces and complex patterns of imagery. Do not overlook the importance of colour. All these things have significance for the structure, as well as the themes, of the novels. They also symbolise the chief motivations and personal traits of the characters.

Read what the critics have to say on the novels—but read them critically. Do not blindly and unthinkingly accept the views of others. If you agree with what a critic has to say about the novel you are studying, remember to acknowledge his or her authorship of the idea if you use it.

Remember that critical commentaries are best used as a catalyst to your own critical thought.

Most of all, remember that achieving a thorough working knowledge of a novel by Fitzgerald (or any author) requires a lot of close reading, rereading and evaluation. The author has set out deliberately to encourage you to make assumptions and predictions about his characters which further experience requires you to revise. None of this can be achieved in the last weeks leading up to any examination which seeks to test your understanding.

Step 2: Research and analysis

Research past examination papers and examiners' comments. Your librarian will assist you. (If you have time, your research should extend to university questions on the text that you are studying.) By doing this, you will familiarise yourself with the examination format and the type of questions to expect. Beware, however! Do not presume that the questions in your exam will be the same as in past papers, or that they will be restricted to the same characters, themes, or major chapters and events. Remember that the syllabus is comprehensive, and you cannot cut corners by anticipating the examiner's focus. You must know the novel which you are studying so well that you can answer a full range of questions.

Step 3: Organisation and learning

Organise your class notes, highlighting and abbreviating them. Learn selected quotes. Write your practice essays within the time allocated to the novel question in the exam.

Step 4 : The exam itself

Follow all instructions carefully.

Allocate your time accurately.

Make the most of your reading time. Read carefully through the whole paper. Check the number of questions which you are required to answer. Identify the types of questions, the compulsory and optional sections, and the allocation of marks. Then reread the paper and choose your questions.

Having made your choice, be committed to it!

Do not make a rash decision to omit a section or a question, or part of a question. To do so will place undue pressure on your performance in the other questions, or the remaining parts of the individual question.

For every question selected, set aside one minute to jot down or plan your attack. Note particularly the individual parts of questions that have two or more prongs, so that you can write a thoughtful discussion of each of them and of their relationship to each other. Assess the relevance and demands of each phrase in the question and any words which define the focus of your answer. To assist your own focus, underline key words and phrases in the question.

Plan your attack. You must write a sound introduction which clearly states your point of view. It should also provide a guide to the structure of your argument.

The body of your essay must be a logical, developed discussion which illustrates and supports your point of view.

Your conclusion must be balanced and logical, preferably drawing together the main points of your argument and repeating the topic with the emphasis which your discussion has given it. Always write some form of conclusion.

Avoid these common pitfalls:

*   Covering only a portion of the novel or of a character's development when the question demands a consideration of the whole. To cover a larger range of events and issues in a long story, select four or five key moments and concentrate your discussion upon these.

*   Writing about only one of a group of characters when the question asks you to consider the whole. As you study the characters, assign them to categories so that you understand their development and interaction. Some useful categories (and the characters of Fitzgerald's work fall into more than one) are: established wealth (the Buchanans); the aspiring *nouveau riche*, the parvenus (Gatsby); the fringe-dwellers of rich society (Nick Carraway and Myrtle Wilson); the dispirited poor (the new servant class of George Wilson); the poor Middle West

farmers (Henry Gatz); the bohemian class (the actresses, directors and chorus girls); the criminals (Wolfshiem); the entrepreneurs; the defeated; and the triumphant.

- Retelling or summarising the plot of the story instead of analysing the significance of individual moments and events to the matters raised in the question.
- Drifting away from the main focus of the question and the mainstream of your argument; becoming sidetracked by minor points.
- Providing so much evidence and so long a quote that the point supported becomes lost in the detail.
- Relying on quotes to state rather than to support your point of view.
- Ignoring the second half of the question.
- Writing descriptively instead of analytically.

3

The novel in close-up

Chapter I

A father's advice

Nick commences his narration of the events of the novel with an acknowledgment of the source of the perspective with which he will recount them—a perspective founded upon the advice of his father given to him in 'younger and more vulnerable years' (7). What is the essence of that advice? The need to restrain criticism of others? To give others the benefit of the doubt? To remember that people's characters and lives are influenced—even perhaps formed—by the advantages they have or lack in the world? To listen whilst reserving judgment? To tolerate human foibles? To be generous-spirited?

> (7) '... I'm inclined to reserve all judgements ...'

NOTE

- the attractiveness of Nick to other people as a result of his following his father's advice

  > (7) '... a habit that has opened up ...'

- the accusation levied at Nick in college, and the reason for it
- Nick's judgment of the nature of the intimacies shared with him by others
- Nick's own assessment of himself as a person blessed at birth with a disproportionate sense of 'fundamental decencies' (7).

CONSIDER

- the irony in Nick's readiness to judge the intimacies of others in the same breath as he insists upon his reserve of judgment

- the possible importance to the novel of Nick's attraction of 'abnormal' personalities and the retrospective irony of this in his appeal to Gatsby
- the hopefulness which Nick preserves about life and people

  (7) 'Reserving judgements is a matter of infinite hope.'

- the defined limits of Nick's tolerance: do they prevent his becoming obsequious from the reader's point of view, preserving common humanity with which the reader can identify?
- the significance of the introduction of water imagery in Nick's reference to the 'wet marshes' upon which confidence can be founded—and the first suggestion in the novel of the geography of the East at the time of its first settlement by Europeans
- the significance of Nick's early admission of defeat in the East and his reference to its having enlisted him on another front—arguably as moral commentator and guardian—and its curing him of any desire to confront the wild passions of others.

  (8) 'When I came back from the East … I wanted no more …'

The extraordinary man who was Gatsby

Nick's sojourn in the East has taught him to regard his fellow humans with general disgust. The only exception to this is Gatsby. This man represented 'everything for which he had an unaffected scorn' (8), but was also a heroic representation of the possibilities open to a man who directed his personality to realising life's promises.

  (8) 'If personality is an unbroken series …'

What is the effect upon the reader of the combination of positive and negative elements in Nick's summation of Gatsby's character? What are our resulting expectations of Gatsby? Heroism? Eccentricity? Egotism? Optimism? Romanticism? Hopefulness? Sensitivity? Energy? Colour? Affectation? Strength of personality? An extraordinary individuality? What is the effect of Nick's final summation of Gatsby as a victim of his world? As a man whose dreams were destroyed by the 'foul dust' that floated in their wake, is Gatsby both tragic hero —a man set apart from common man—in the power of his dreams, and an Everyman in having dreamt them?

A well-to-do Middle Western family

Having introduced Gatsby, Nick proceeds to introduce himself. He is of good Middle Western stock, from a family so close-knit as to earn the description of 'clan'. It is a family with its own mythology, laying claim to a noble lineage from the Dukes of Buccleuch, but in fact from a more ignominious background.

Nick's great-uncle was a substitute in the Civil War and the founder of the wholesale hardware business which Nick's father continues to carry on. It is a family that knows the nobility of service. Nick himself, in his participation in the Great War, has continued the war service of family members. How could the effect of this service be described? As making the young man restless, and disenchanted with his familiar milieu? Has his war service created the desire to explore and to exploit fully the possibilities of his youth and of life? Has it made him determined to carve out his future in the new commercialism which was engulfing America in the spring of 1922?

CONSIDER

- the relevance to a biography of an individual of the reference to the Civil War. What thematic concerns are foreshadowed by the reference to America's own revolution and to the roots of American democracy?
- the significance of Nick's resemblance of his great-uncle. Has he too been a pioneer consolidating or extending the foundations of his family?
- the symbolic meaning of the painting which hangs in Nick's father's office
- the symbolic significance of Nick's commencement of his journey to what he thought would be a promising new life in the warmth of spring
- the powerful emphasis upon migration
- the contrast between the country which Nick left and the city to which he came.

(9) '… I had just left …'

A shared house in a commuting town

Nick rejects the practicality of taking rooms in the city, in favour of a shared house in a commuting town. Fate—in the form of the transfer of his intended house-mate—sees Nick taking up residence in the shabby house on his own.

(9) '… a weather-beaten cardboard bungalow …'

How suggestive is his description of his new home? Does it imply financial hardship? Economy? Realism? Is it the novel's first image of a darker underside to the rich glamour of the times? Or does it link up with the earlier reference to the 'foul dust'? Is there sadness in the dog's running away? Is it sad that Nick is largely alone, without the support of his extended family back home? What finishes this loneliness?

NOTE

- the dog's running away reiterates the motif of escapism first introduced by Nick's abandonment of his Middle Western home town
- Nick's purchase of an old Dodge motor vehicle—an accessory for his new life
- the migrant Finnish woman who does Nick's cooking.

The Great Gatsby

CONSIDER

- the strength of the pathfinder image

  (9) 'I was a guide, a pathfinder ...'

- the importance of the second reference to America's past, further back this time to the era of the first settlers. Why does Fitzgerald place Nick in the tradition of America's pioneers?
- the landscape's echoing of Nick's newfound joy and sense of freedom and, most of all, his sense of hope, of an open-ended promise of success

  (9) 'And so with the sunshine ...'

Is Nick reborn at this moment—from a disenchanted to an optimistic young man? Is he at this point overwhelmed by the sense of his own life's possibilities? Is the warmth of the sunshine his baptism into a new life?

Nick changes from repatriated soldier to a student of banking. His bibles for his new religion stand red and gold on his shelves. What is the significance of the simile he uses to describe them?

  (10) '... they stood on my shelf ...'

These tomes are full of 'shining secrets' of how to become a new Midas, Morgan and Maecenas. They are to be Nick's new focus, his guide to the single window of materialism through which he now views his world. Is there a suggestion of magic here? A suggestion of new codes and new formulas for success and happiness to be learned by the as-yet-uninitiated Nick?

The Eggs

As chance would have it, Nick has rented his house in one of the strangest communities in North America. What are the effects of his descriptions of it as 'riotous' and its land formations as 'natural curiosities'(10)? What expectations about the citizens of this special community are built up by these descriptions? Bohemianism? Eccentricity? Extreme wealth? Self-indulgence?

CONSIDER

- the fertility symbolism of the Eggs
- the significance of the further reminders of the early Americans and of early America in the reference to Columbus
- the significance and relevance of the barnyard image.

West Egg

Nick's house is at the very tip of West Egg. Is there a suggestion here that he can only cling to the periphery of this community? The house is squeezed between

12

two huge places that 'rented for twelve or fifteen thousand a season'. The one on his right was Gatsby's house.

Gatsby's house—an imitation of some Hôtel de Ville in Normandy

There is a rawness, a newness, about Gatsby's house, symbolised in the sparseness of the ivy beard which it wears. It is all show and ostentation, with its enormous tower, marble swimming pool and forty-plus acres of lawn and garden. The latter provides part of the vista that Nick obtains from his $80-a-month 'eyesore' (11). What implied comment on the egalitarianism (or lack of it) of this new frontier is presented by the contrast between Gatsby's and Nick's homes? Is Gatsby's home an unqualified statement of success? Or does its imagery suggest some doubts?

The Buchanans' home

The house of Daisy and Tom is across the 'courtesy bay' from Gatsby's. It is a 'palace' (11). Daisy is Nick's second cousin once removed; her husband Tom was a college acquaintance. Nick's narrative really begins, as he says, when he drives to their home to take up from where they had left off after spending two days together after the war in Chicago.

The Buchanans

Tom is a very physical man, known in New Haven for his football prowess. By the age of twenty-one, he had been national hero and achieved all the excellence a young man might desire. What was left for him? More of the same? His own ennui? His own restlessness? Why couldn't the enormous wealth that he shared with his family save him from directionlessness? What was he trying to achieve by the extravagant gesture of bringing down East a string of polo ponies from Lake Forest? Does the gesture define his sense of superiority? Or hide a sense of inferiority? Does he display a personal need for a prop to his existence? Is he irretrievably lost in a mountain of money? Is he cut off from the basic pioneering values upon which his country was built?

The Buchanans' reason for coming East is itself a mystery. Before seeking the pleasures of New York they had tested those of France for a year, and then had drifted aimlessly wherever 'people played polo and were rich together' (11). Daisy assures Nick on the telephone that their move East was a permanent arrangement—yet he doubts this. Why?

Q (12) '... I felt that Tom would drift on forever seeking ...'

A warm, windy evening and a Georgian colonial mansion

On a warm, windy evening, Nick drives over to the Buchanans' house. Its grandeur makes Gatsby's pale into insignificance. Its owner—Tom Buchanan—stands on its front porch with a confident stance which encompasses his whole universe.

NOTE

- the quarter-mile of the Buchanan lawns
- their private beach
- the brightness of the vines which cling to the Buchanan walls
- Tom's proprietorial air and his riding attire, his defensiveness and simmering aggression.

CONSIDER

- the possible social, cultural, and philosophical conflicts suggested in the different architectural styles of the two homes. Does the Buchanans' home link them with the Establishment? Does Gatsby's home link him with revolutionaries?
- the symbolic significance of the sundials as reminders in the Buchanans' home of the passing of time
- the reflected gold of the french windows which line the front of the Buchanan house
- the symbolic suggestiveness of the 'burning gardens'(12). Is this place a corrupted paradise?

Tom Buchanan

Tom is a man whose physique and bearing exude strength and confidence. A blond 30-year-old, he is notable for the cruelty of his mouth, the aggressive arrogance of his eyes, and the cruelty of his body. What is suggested by his dress? Is he a symbol of the fascism which was to grip Europe a decade later with the rise of Nazism? How popular was he at New Haven? And after? How comfortable had Nick felt as a member of the same senior society?

    (12) '... there were men at New Haven ...'

What are the words with which Tom greets Nick?

    (12) ' "I've got a nice place ..." '

What does Fitzgerald achieve by describing the restlessness of Tom's eyes? Does it evoke suspicious watchfulness on Tom's part? Defensiveness? Lack of direction? A sense of indescribable inner restlessness? An abundance of energy which lacks a focus? With his sunken Italian garden, half-acre of roses, and motorboat, Tom is surrounded by conspicuous wealth and the symbols of heady indulgence, purchased by him from a very respectable and equally rich vendor—Demaine, the oil man. Nick follows Tom inside the house at his order.

A rosy-coloured space

The room they enter is rose-coloured and airy; its windows gleam white against the grass, which threatens to come inside. What does the last detail suggest? That everything, even here, is under threat? That the earth wishes to reclaim its own? That even the grandest things are transient?

A breeze blows through the room and twists the curtains into flags, carrying them up to the frosted wedding-cake ceiling; the wine-coloured rug ripples like the sea. The scene is one of all-engulfing restlessness. It is also full of resonances: the retrospective image of the sailing ships, caught by the same breeze as they entered the sound for the first time, combines with the prospective image of the pool of blood which is to be Gatsby's fate. Is the shadow ominous?

Daisy and Jordan

The room is dominated by a couch which appears to bear up the two young women who lie recumbent on it, as if they were suspended above the ordinary in a balloon. Their dresses are rippled by the same wind. Their appearance is of two angels or birds who have just landed after a flight around the house. Is the suggestion one of goddesses? What is the effect on the scene of the negative sounds which also attract Nick's attention here—the 'whip and snap' of the curtains and the 'groan of the picture on the wall' (13)? And of the 'boom' which attends Tom's shutting out the breeze?

Jordan Baker is haughtily superior in her motionless pose.

Q (14) 'She was extended full length …'

What ideas are introduced into the characterisation of Jordan by the simile of balance which describes her poise? Superiority? A notion of judgment? (This judgment becomes retrospectively ironic when her dishonesty is subsequently revealed.) Does the reference to the view that she might have had out of the side of her eyes suggest dishonesty? A certain personal shiftiness? A moral connection to Tom and his flashing, restless eyes?

Daisy is equally affected and self-conscious. Her action of leaning forward—ever so slightly—is studied and unspontaneous. Is this the first mark of her insincerity? Her shallowness? What do her first words to Nick suggest about her?

Q (14) '"I'm p-paralysed with happiness."'

Is Daisy herself a cliché? Are her feelings false? Do they lack warmth and sincerity? Her laugh is attractive, alluring. Is it genuine? What is its effect upon

Nick? Is this effect calculated? Why does Nick so readily dismiss others' criticism of it as 'irrelevant'?

CONSIDER

- the symbolic suggestion of Jordan Baker's fluttering lips (14). Are they powerfully symbolic of her dishonesty? Does her restlessness align her with Tom Buchanan?
- the basis of Nick's attraction to Jordan: is the degree of her self-sufficiency potentially dangerous?
- the musical quality of Daisy's voice and the brightness, yet also the sadness, in her face. Is there enough here to suggest inner turmoil? A disguised sense of loss?
- Daisy's fateful attractiveness, the strength of which must explain Gatsby's infatuation with her

    (14–15) 'Her face was sad and lovely with bright things in it …'

- Nick's exaggeration of the desolation of Chicago in Daisy's absence
- the symbolic suggestiveness and thematic significance of the mourning images which colour Nick's account to Daisy of Chicago
- Nick's readiness to play Daisy's game, to feed her ego and sense of self-importance.

    (15) '"The whole town is desolate."'

The baby

Daisy tells Nick that he ought to see 'the baby'. What can be deduced from her failure to refer to the child by name, and from her failure to remember whether Nick had seen the three-year-old? What of Tom's interruption of the conversation? Does his own daughter hold no interest for him? What is to be made of his 'restless hovering' (15)? And of the controlled derision with which he responds to Nick's explanation of his employment as a bond man? Is he more polite to Jordan at her rejection of the cocktail which is brought in from the pantry for each of them?

Jordan Baker

Slender and small-breasted, Jordan is the quintessential flapper—a young modern woman with the erect carriage of a military cadet. Is she a trainee in Tom's elitist army of the aggrieved, suspicious and restless? For what is her face remarkable?

    (16) 'She was a slender …'

Why does Jordan mirror Tom in her contempt for Nick? What is his response when she introduces Gatsby's name into their conversation?

Dinner and candles

Tom leads Nick into dinner as assertively as he ushered him into the house.

> (16) '... wedging his tense arm ...'

Is Tom a power freak, a man who must be always in control?

Daisy exclaims at the candles which adorn the dinner table and promptly snaps them out with her fingers. Why? Is it a symbolic rejection of the romanticism that they suggest? Could it be an act (viewed retrospectively) in response to the mention of Gatsby's name? Her conversation is without true content—is a day waited for really missed? Does the passing of time escape her so literally?

NOTE

- Jordan's yawning at the tedium of yet another dinner
- Daisy's helplessness at the mention of plans
- Daisy's display of her bruised little finger and her altercation with Tom about her description of him
- Nick's observations upon the coldness of the chatter of Daisy and Jordan and the impersonality of their eyes

> (17) 'Sometimes she and Miss Baker talked at once ...'

- the contrast which Nick draws between the passing of evenings in the West and here, in the Buchanans' East.

Nick complains to Daisy about the feeling of barbarity which her sophistication engenders in him. Yet, before she can respond, Tom interjects with a vicious condemnation of the civilisation to which Nick aspires.

> (18) '"Civilization's going to pieces ..."'

Tom supports his point by a reference to Goddard's work describing the rise of the coloured races (a veiled reference by Fitzgerald to *The Rising Tide of Colour* by Lothrop Stoppard). He has embraced as scientific its thesis that the white race is soon to be submerged, a race which he believes is innately superior and chosen by nature to rule. Does this explain Tom's aggression? Fully? (Even, as it seems, to Daisy?) Or is there a suggestion that its basis is more complicated than this?

Tom interrupts Jordan's suggestion that he ought to live in California to pronounce his racial theory. Is it significant that he includes Daisy amongst the Nordic elite only with a desultory nod?

The telephone interruption

When Tom's deliberations are interrupted by the ringing of the telephone, Daisy seizes the chance to narrate the story of the butler's nose. Is the story merely a light diversion? Does her and her friend's interest in the butler's nose show the

emptiness of their lives? Is the story also significant for the vignette it provides of their society's exploitation and then discarding of people?

As Daisy tells her story, her face is caressed with light.

> (19) 'For a moment the last sunshine fell ...'

Is she really the glowing princess? Is Tom her gaoler?

As Tom deserts them to take the phone-call, Daisy speaks of Tom as a rose, with a warmth which suggests that she is reaching out to him. Why, then, does she suddenly throw her napkin on the table and move into the house? Has she exhausted her pretence of happiness? Or of unconcern?

Tom's New York woman

In the absence of both Tom and Daisy, Jordan explains to Nick why she strains to hear the conversation in the other room—it is commonly known that Tom has 'got some woman in New York' (20). At that, the others return. Daisy, with forced gaiety, speaks of a lost nightingale which might be the singing bird on the lawn, of romance, and of a planned tour after dinner for Nick of the stables. Yet her true sadness is only too evident.

NOTE

- the further reference to ships coming over from the Continent—an echo of the East's history
- the pointless relighting of the candles
- Nick's embarrassed avoidance of all eyes
- the consciousness of them all of the 'fifth guest' (Tom's woman) at their table
- Nick's instinct to telephone the police.

Are the events of the dinner an instruction for Nick of the darker underside of the Buchanans' wealthy lives? Is this also the effect of the image used to describe the entry of Jordan and Tom into the library?

> (21) 'Tom and Miss Baker ... strolled back into the library ...'

Is it significant that Tom is accompanied by his disciple, perhaps to jointly pursue further tomes on the rise or fall of civilisation?

Daisy's confession

Daisy and Nick move to the porch and sit in the twilight together. Daisy confesses to cynicism, and even the topic of her daughter cannot move her from her torpor. She describes the moments after the child's birth (in the absence of Tom) and her wish for her daughter—that she be a 'beautiful little fool'.

> (22) '"And I hope she'll be a fool ..."'

Her bitterness and emptiness are indeed profound.

(22) ' "You see I think everything's terrible ..." '

Nick doubts Daisy's sincerity. Why? Why does he feel that the whole evening has been 'a trick' (22)?

Sharing the news

Daisy and Nick return to a scene of domestic bliss—Jordan reading aloud from the *Saturday Evening Post* to Tom. Her voice is a soothing murmur. She and Tom are joined by the glow of the lamplight on Tom's boots, on the autumn yellow of her hair, and on the gentle flutter of her arm muscles. Jordan leaves off as Nick and Daisy enter. After commanding their attention, she announces that, it being ten o'clock, she will retire to bed. Daisy explains that Jordan is to play in the tournament at Westchester the next day, causing Nick to realise that the girl he sees before him is Jordan Baker the golfer, whose face has stared out from the pages of sporting life at Asheville and Hot Springs and Palm Beach. He recalls some suggestion of scandal about its owner, a 'story', but abandons its details to the dimness of memory.

As Jordan bids Nick goodnight, Daisy speaks of arranging her marriage to Nick, and the ploys which she will use to bring them together.

CONSIDER

- the symbolic and thematic suggestiveness of the author's selection of Tom's boots and Jordan's arm muscles and assertive body with its restless knee movements for specific descriptive comment. Is the suggestion one of innate violence hidden by a deceptively serene exterior?
- Jordan's command for silence with the uplift of her hand. Is she also a power freak? Is this gesture militaristic?
- the ploys canvassed by Daisy aimed at fostering the relationship between Nick and Jordan. Are they indicative of the games played by members of her set?
- the details of Jordan's restlessness: the lack of a controlling family influence provided by an aunt who is 'a thousand years old' (23); her running around the country; the ironic antidote to such restlessness proffered by Daisy
- Jordan's common background with Daisy—a white girlhood spent in Louisville.

Gossip

The attention of the evening turns to Nick and the gossip, which Daisy and Tom have heard from three sources, that Nick is engaged to be married. Nick explains the facts: that he had had a relationship with an old friend, but that he was not going to be 'rumoured into marriage' (24). His explanation confirms that the gossip was founded on fact. What else does it confirm? The power of public

opinion? That the Buchanans' world is driven by gossip and innuendo? That the public is only too ready to give credence to such gossip? That there is an element of truth in any rumour?

Nick's sadness for his hosts

Nick is touched by the interest of his hosts in his personal life. It made them 'less remotely rich'. The farewell scene which his softened imagination dreams up is not realised, however. Daisy does not run out of the house with the baby in her arms. Tom's personal image is enlarged for Nick, not because he has a 'woman in New York' but because he was depressed by a book.

> (25) 'Something was making him nibble at the edge of stale ideas ...'

For all his physicality, Tom is plagued by spiritual or ideological emptiness. The dangers of Tom's intellectual excursions—perhaps of gossip or even of the fact of existing in the world of East Egg—is hinted at by the blood-red of the petrol-pumps, which reflect the light of deep summer as Nick makes his way home. The atmosphere is funereal and disturbing: wings beat in the trees, the earth seems engulfed by a persistent organ sound of frogs, the moon is itself shadowed by the form of a cat. Are these images also omens of evil? Are they full of sinister suggestiveness? Do they foreshadow the events that are to engulf the novel? How satisfactory are they as an overture to the tableau that then unfolds of Nick's neighbour?

A figure emerges from the shadows

Gatsby emerges from the shadows to stand on his lawn —in mimicry of Tom's earlier stance on the Buchanans' porch. Gatsby's eyes strain to the stars.

> (24) 'Something in his leisurely movements ...'

Is this the attitude and behaviour of a confident man? A romantic? A dreamer? What is to be made of Gatsby's subsequent gesture: the stretching out of his arms toward the 'dark water'(24)? What is the combined effect of Gatsby's trembling and the 'unquiet darkness' which remains when he vanishes, as if he had been a ghost? What is the meaning of the minute green light to which Gatsby's arms had reached? Compare this reference to the green light with the references to it at the end of the novel (171). Does it symbolise the infinitely distant hope for personal fulfilment that motivates all who dare to dream?

Examining the issues

1. Examine the reasons why Nick turns his back on the Middle West to explore the new world of the East. Is this journey a rite of passage, his initiation into the morality of the postwar adult world? Is it his journey from innocence to

experience? Can he be described as innocent when he has experienced first-hand the horrors of the war? Has the war already transformed him into an adventurer who is in search of new challenges?

2. The Buchanans represent the Establishment. They are beautiful and their lives are glamorous. Or is there something sinister under the surface?

3. The first chapter is dominated by two set scenes: two beautiful women in white occupying each end of an enormous couch, the only stationary object in a breeze-filled room; and Gatsby, his arms outstretched towards the dark water and a minute, single, distant green light.
    * What ideas are dramatically presented here?
    * What is the effect of the association of Gatsby with the stars and the moon?
    * How do the references to birds define the romantic vision which Gatsby has of Daisy? Does the author hint at its ephemeral nature?
    * Tom Buchanan is ready for war—but against what and in support of what? Does he know?
    * How deeply felt is Myrtle's presence in Daisy's home and at her dinner table?
    * What images of death pervade this chapter?
    * Examine the images of gold and roses which colour Nick's narrative in this chapter. How do they contribute to Daisy Buchanan's characterisation?
    * How is the atmosphere of the Buchanans' dinner party changed by Myrtle Wilson's telephone call?

4. Nick describes the forces which destroyed Gatsby's dream as 'the foul dust [which] floated in [their] wake'(8). Does Fitzgerald bring together here two symbols of the antitheses which dominate the novel's themes and inform its characters? Can the dust be identified with the powerful symbol of spiritual emptiness defined in T. S. Eliot's poem 'The Wasteland'? Is the floating behaviour of that dust a mockery of the habit of water, the one element that is the antidote to such sterility, the symbol of regeneration and fresh life?

Chapter II

The Valley of Ashes

The Valley of Ashes occupies the expanse of flat land that lies between West Egg and New York. Is it the guardian of the city? Does it represent the city's moral and spiritual condition to all those who pass by on their way to the city? It is a 'fantastic farm' (26), a parody of the once green fertile farms that the pioneers had established after the first settlement of America. It is a landscape replete with its own God—the impaired eyes of a Doctor T. J. Eckleburg, the advertising bill-board of a long-dead oculist. It is a landscape peopled by ash-grey men who tend the grey cars which crawl along the invisible track to stop in the ashen air. This

is 'a dumping ground' of the hopeless and of the rejected, imprisoned on one side by its own foul river. This is also the home of Tom's mistress.

Tom Buchanan's mistress

Nick reports on the gossipmongers' universal insistence upon the reality of Tom's mistress. Nick unexpectedly meets her, as Tom interrupts their rail journey to New York to drag him across the ash heaps to George Wilson's garage. It is a Sunday afternoon. How could the manner of Tom's request be described? Cajoling? Violently insistent? Bullying?

The garage of George B. Wilson

The third in a line of premises occupying a small yellow-brick block at the edge of the wasteland houses George Wilson's garage. The interior cries poverty and has its own creature occupant—an old dusty Ford crouching in the corner. Nick's imagination rejects its dirty reality. It must surely, he concludes, be a blind to rich apartments concealed overhead.

      (27) 'It had occurred to me that this shadow of a garage ...'

The proprietor stands at its door, wiping his hands on a piece of waste. Blond like Tom, he is spiritually a total contrast.

      (27) 'He was a blond, spiritless man, anaemic ...'

What is significant about his eyes? Why is the hope in them dim?

NOTE

- the deal which Tom seems to be in the process of engineering for George
- Tom's coldness
- George Wilson's powerlessness against Tom's anger.

A sensuously fleshy woman

George Wilson's wife is an arresting character, not in her beauty (as Daisy is) but in her vitality.

      (28) 'She was in the middle thirties ...'

She walks through her husband 'as if he were a ghost', to face Tom squarely, before giving orders to the man whom she is betraying.

CONSIDER

- the effectiveness of the ghost image which conveys George Wilson's lack of consequence for all those present
- Tom's demand to Myrtle to get on the next train

- Tom's dismissal of George as a 'dumb' man (29), and his disgust at the wasteland itself
- the significance of the scrawny Italian child playing with torpedoes along the railway track
- the ironic reminder that in four days' time it was to be the Fourth of July. Do the Valley of Ashes, and the lives of its inhabitants, represent a perversion of the values of American society that are represented by this day of celebration?

The other life of Myrtle Wilson

Having exchanged her dark-blue dress for one of brown figured muslin, Myrtle Wilson, the mistress, takes on a new persona. What part is played in this by her purchase of the gossip newspaper, *Town Tattle*, and a moving picture magazine? Do these two items sum up the morality of the world she has adopted, its love of gossip and its need for escapism? Does she engage our sympathy by her more womanly purchases of a jar of cold cream and some cheap perfume? And in her selectiveness when it comes to the taxi which is to convey her to her rendezvous? What does her purchase of the puppy suggest? A longing for status? A desire for a substitute child? A residual innocence? A need to be loved, or to show love?

The dog vendor is a shabby, grey man who looks decidedly like John D. Rockefeller—one of the richest men of the times. Is this Fitzgerald's symbolic prediction of the Depression that will end the gay lives of many of the rich at the end of the decade?

Fifth Avenue

Warm and 'almost pastoral' on the summer afternoon, Fifth Avenue is at its best—a stark contrast to the world of the wasteland not far distant. What is significant in Nick's reference to the 'great flock of white sheep' which he almost expects to see arrive around the corner? Is the expectation built upon an intuitive tuning in to the hopes and dreams of the first American pioneers for the New World that they had come to establish? Does Fifth Avenue represent the apotheosis of these dreams?

Nick is pressured by both Tom and Myrtle to come up to their apartment in a 'long white cake of apartment-houses'. What can be made of their shape? An ironic imitation of a wedding cake? What of Myrtle's attempt at matchmaking? In her attempt to team Nick up with her sister, does she ironically parallel Daisy's plans for Nick and Jordan?

The apartment

The apartment itself is characterised by an attempt to put as much tapestried furniture as possible into the smallest space. It is overlooked (in mockery, perhaps, of the god of the Valley of Ashes) by its own goddess—a portrait of an old lady,

which at first impression looks like a hen sitting on a 'blurred rock'. It has its own social and moral bibles—several copies of the *Town Tattle* and a copy of *Simon Called Peter*—and its own (locked) liquor cupboard. To it, on account of the dog, Myrtle adds a saucer of milk; all afternoon, a dog biscuit decomposes in it. What is the atmosphere created here? One of indulgence? A sensual enclave? Cheerfulness (at least while the sun cheers the rooms)? A private speakeasy? Nick is sent away by a ruse to allow Myrtle and Tom private time in the bedroom: what judgment on this is provided by Nick's subsequent criticism of *Simon Called Peter*?

The guests arrive

Catherine, Myrtle's sister, is a 'worldly girl of about thirty'. Her red hair and her double eyebrows make a caricature of her face. She is the not-so-perfect flapper. What is to be made of her living arrangements—with a girlfriend in a hotel? Is there a suggestion that she is more than a party girl? A prostitute, perhaps?

Mr Chester McKee is 'a pale, feminine man from the flat below' (32). He too is flawed, with the remnant of shaving cream on his face. His claim to fame is as the photographer who had enlarged the picture of Myrtle's mother to its present state of absurdity.

Mrs McKee is 'shrill, languid, handsome and horrible' (32). Her only claim to fame is the number of times (one hundred and twenty-seven) which her husband had photographed her since they had been married. Does this suggest a dearth of other clients, perhaps? Or Mr McKee's obsession with his wife?

Another costume change

Myrtle changes to an elaborate afternoon dress of cream-coloured chiffon; this brings about a parallel change in her poise. She adopts a superior air to match the suggestiveness of wealth in the dress. Why is the natural vitality which she exhibited in the garage sacrificed to this new affectation? What is the author's message? That the flapper (whether it be Myrtle or Daisy or Jordan whose dress she copied) is incapable of natural vitality? That the sensuality of the real woman is submerged in the artifice of the woman of rich fashion? That to become one involves an abandonment of the values, as well as the dress, of the other?

Q (33) 'Her laughter, her gestures, her assertions ...'

In deriding Mrs Eberhardt, is Myrtle also deriding her own class? Does this subtract from the significance of her comments upon the power of money in America of 1922 or add to it? Why would her photographer guest find it hard to capture her in her present light?

- yet another reminder of the first settlement of Long Island in Mr McKee's references to his photographs of Montauk Point
- Catherine's transmission to Nick of the gossip that Gatsby is a cousin of Kaiser Wilhelm and derives his money from that source, and her revelation that she is 'scared of him' (35)

> (35) '"I'd hate to have him get anything …"'

- Mrs McKee's persistent search for subjects for her husband's photographic skills
- Tom's mockery of Chester McKee's request for an introduction to Long Island society in his suggestion that Chester should approach Myrtle for a letter of introduction
- the closeness of George Wilson to the surface of Tom's subconscious.

Catherine reveals to Nick the reasons why Tom is unable to marry Myrtle—Daisy is a Catholic and will not give him a divorce. Nick, however, knows that Daisy is not a Catholic. What is Nick's response to this elaborate lie on Tom's part? Why does he suggest that, in the event of the two lovers marrying, they would be better to go to Europe for a while rather than West? What is the significance of the reminder at this stage of the novel of the simple home-town values of the West?

Catherine also confides in Nick her awful experiences in Monte Carlo. For a moment, the later afternoon light 'bloomed' in the window (36).

Lucille McKee and Myrtle Wilson compare notes about their courtship by men who were 'below' them. Lucille announces that she was able to avoid the 'little tyke' who pursued her; Myrtle decries the fact that she was not so fortunate.

> (37) '"I married him because I thought … I knew right away I made a mistake …"'

For eleven years after the event, Catherine tells Nick, Myrtle has lived with George over the garage and Tom is the 'first sweetie' that she has had (37).

A second bottle of whisky

As the party-goers imbibe their second bottle of whisky, Nick's desire to escape to the 'soft twilight' of the park increases. Yet he is held 'as if with ropes' to his chair by his entanglement in a strident argument (37). He is simultaneously enchanted and repelled by his experience.

> (37) 'I was within and without …'

What impression of this lifestyle remains with the reader? Similar enchantment to that felt by Nick? Disgust at the emotional and physical ugliness of it all? Surprise at the frank revelation of dark emotions and deep regrets? At the strength of the characters' incipient unhappiness? At their drunkenness? At their insensitivity to others?

Myrtle's confession of her first meeting with Tom

Spontaneously and with her breath warmed by whisky, Myrtle narrates to Nick the events of her first meeting with Tom.

NOTE

- it was a chance meeting on the train
- she was on her way to spend the night in New York with her sister; Tom had on a dress suit and patent leather shoes
- he had brushed her arm with his shirt front when they had come into the station, and shortly after, she had hardly been able to contain her excitement when she got into a taxi with him
- her rationalisation of it had been that 'You can't live forever' (38).

What is to be made of the artificial laughter with which Myrtle accompanies her story? Insincerity? Embarrassment? An attempt to hide regret in pretended hilarity? Is her intended shopping spree the next day a similar distraction? Myrtle adds an artificial wreath for her mother's grave to a shopping list that includes a massage, a new dress, a collar for the dog and an ashtray; is this symptomatic of her loss of true values?

As the evening wears on to nine and then ten o'clock, the inhabitants of the apartment appear increasingly discomfited: even in sleep Mr McKee's clamped fists seem to suggest that he continues a private war; the dog groans faintly in the smoky fog; people (unnamed and nameless) disappear, lose each other, find each other, and repeat the process. The general tedium is at last broken at midnight by the argument between Tom and Myrtle over Myrtle's right to utter Daisy's name. Why does Tom prohibit such an action with the violent act of breaking Myrtle's nose with his hand? Is it an act of despair? A deliberate assertion of his power? A statement of his lack of any genuine feeling for Myrtle? An expression of deep ennui? The scene is energised by the aftermath of Tom's violence.

> (39) 'Then there were bloody towels upon the bathroom floor ...'

Nick and Chester McKee seize the opportunity to make their escape. Nick's last image of McKee is of a man sitting up in bed in his underwear, surveying a great portfolio of his work. Is it significant that one photograph is entitled 'Beauty and the Beast' and another 'Loneliness'? Do they reflect upon the relationships of the party-goers upstairs, and the reasons for their being together?

The night concludes for Nick in Pennsylvania Station, where he is waiting for the four o'clock train.

Examining the issues

1. Discuss the strata of society portrayed at Myrtle's party. Why has Tom Buchanan chosen to be a part of it?

2. Analyse the techniques used by Fitzgerald to portray character in this chapter. How important to this are the images and events of violence?

3. How does the author interweave Tom's and Myrtle's consciousness of the marriage partners whom they are betraying in their affair?

4. To what extent might Myrtle's love-nest be described as an exercise in bad taste and pretentiousness?

5. What is Daisy's presence in Myrtle's love-nest? Does she intrude as significantly as Myrtle had done at Daisy's dinner party in the previous chapter?

6. What symbolic significance can be attributed to Myrtle's costume changes?

7. In this chapter, Myrtle is comically affected in her manner and speech. Does her vitality nevertheless save her from being ludicrous?

8. How do the events of Chapter II, the observations of the characters, and the setting of Myrtle's apartment develop the novel's analysis of a society founded upon money?

9. What ironic parallels can be drawn between Tom's mistress and his wife? Apart from violence, do they get anything out of the relationship? Affection? Lust? Status? Do both women equally engage our sympathies?

10. How important in this scene is the characters' consciousness or interest in scandal?

11. How important to the development of character and of theme is the biblical imagery and symbolism which colours this chapter? Is the Valley of Ashes a symbol of purgatory? Are the eyes of T. J. Eckleburg those of a corrupted deity? Is the portrait of Myrtle's mother a replacement for a portrait of Christ of the Sacred Heart, or of Mary, the mother of Christ? Is there a Madonna image attached to Myrtle? Is she the Fallen Woman personified? Is the washing of people's feet an echo of Christ's washing of the feet of the disciples? Do the images and symbols remind us of the moral standard against which these characters are to be judged, even if they have abandoned it themselves?

12. What judgment of George Wilson's significance (or lack of it) in his world is provided by the position of his garage, on the edge of the wasteland and next to nothing? Is his life a nightmare in which his identity and feelings are lost in swirls of annihilating dust? Is he emotionally, physically and economically defeated? Is he as much a wreck as the cars in which he deals?

13. Identify the perversions of nature in the wasteland of the Valley of Ashes.

14. What images of death pervade this chapter?

Chapter III

Gatsby's parties

Gatsby's parties enliven the summer nights of West Egg. His blue gardens are ravaged by the party-goers who are ferried by Gatsby's own Rolls Royce between the city and Gatsby's home from nine in the morning until midnight, or are fetched by his bug-like station wagon from the station.

CONSIDER

- the statement about conspicuous consumption symbolised in the crates of oranges and lemons which are turned into a pyramid of pulpless halves in the space of a single weekend.

    Q (41) 'Every Friday five crates of oranges and lemons …'

- the opulence represented by the enormous marquees which were erected each fortnight and adorned with Christmas lights and the buffet tables weighed down with sophisticated food. Do these images of consumerism and sensual pleasures suggest the decadence which contributed to the fall of the Roman Empire?

    Q (41) 'On buffet tables …'

- the meaning of Gatsby's flouting of Prohibition with the erection of a well-stocked bar (with a real brass rail) in the main hall: is he a bootlegger?
- the overt expression of wealth in the employment of a full orchestra to provide the entertainment
- the modernity symbolised by the cars parked five deep in the drive
- the repetition of references to the colour yellow—Gatsby's colour. Is this a powerful statement of his wealth?
- the vulnerability suggested in the image of the moth which is introduced at the beginning of the chapter.

The gypsies

Amongst the party-goers are the gypsies, anonymous girls who float from one group to another, grabbing the limelight for brief moments before being supplanted by others even more beautiful or fascinating. One takes the stage, dancing alone on the canvas platform. Is she a symbol of drunkenness? Lost innocence? Exhibitionism? This performance of Gilda Gray's understudy is the signal for the real party to begin.

No invitation necessary

Nick is unusual in that he attends his first party on Gatsby's invitation—formally delivered by Gatsby's blue-uniformed chauffeur. The others, it seems, have merely turned up.

Q (43) 'People were not invited ...'

Once there, they conduct themselves as if they were at an amusement park. Some come and go without ever speaking to their host.

Lost in swirls and eddies of people

Nick is uncomfortable amongst the crowds at his first party. What observation does he make about the contrast between the numerous young Englishmen and Americans there?

Q (43) 'I was immediately struck ...'

Is Fitzgerald deliberately promoting all things in the New World against the decrepitude of the Old? Nick is convinced that the young Americans are selling 'bonds, or insurance or automobiles' (43): are these the foundations of this new wealth?

Some of Gatsby's guests know so little of him that they cannot assist Nick when he asks where Gatsby is. Escaping from embarrassment into drunkenness, Nick sights Jordan Baker and attaches himself to her. How does she receive him? With contempt or indifference? Is she barely concealing her anger at her recent loss in a tournament? They join a group notable for its members' preservation of their anonymity.

Q (44) 'A tray of cocktails floated at us through the twilight ...'

Party conversation

The three Mr Mumbles and the two girls with yellow hair regale Jordan and Nick with snippets of their party experiences: one of the girls who had ripped her dress at an earlier party had been provided with an expensive replacement by Gatsby; Gatsby always remained aloof; Gatsby was a German spy in the war; Gatsby probably killed a man. Gatsby's stature is enlarged even further for Nick because of the interest he engenders in such simple-minded and unfocused individuals.

Q (45) 'It was testimony ...'

What impression is given by the matching haircolour and hairstyle of the two young women? Anonymity? The submergence of individuality in a common mode (of thinking as well as of appearance)? The dominance of fashion? An illustration of society's supreme emphasis upon externals (as opposed to morality)?

What impression is given when each of the young women's male companions murmurs her name so that it cannot be heard? Are they cheating on their wives? Are they engaging in behaviour (such as drinking alcohol) which is illegal and can ruin their respectable reputations?

Supper is enlivened by the violent and obscene innuendos of Jordan's partner. Has this social milieu abandoned all rules, all sense of propriety?

A search for Gatsby and a meeting with a middle-aged man

Bored by the homogeneous reserve of the East Egg sect who protect their exclusiveness from adulteration by the presence of West Eggers, Jordan escapes with Nick to search for Gatsby. They do not find their host immediately, but come upon a stout, middle-aged man with enormous owl-eyed spectacles, in the library, enthusing over the shelves of real books. Drunk for about a week, he had retreated there in an attempt to sober up. Why does Gatsby's library evoke so much interest? Is it because it is genuine in a sea of fakery? Does it remind us that all the great ideas of civilisation have foundered upon Jazz Age society? Does it echo Tom's despair at the decay of civilisation? Is this bespectacled gentleman the incarnation of the deity of the Valley of Ashes, a corrupt parallel to Christ as God made man?

The dancing begins

The dance floor is a canvas spread out in the garden. The dancers provide a microcosm of society: old men with young girls; superior, self-conscious couples remaining apart from the rest; single girls making their own individualistic way. The music is mixed, and the hilarity increases as the floor is taken over by an Italian tenor, a contralto singing jazz, and a costumed baby act by a pair of stage twins.

Still Gatsby is nowhere to be seen. Nick feels warmed by the quantity of champagne that he has drunk.

Q (48) 'I had taken two finger-bowls of champagne ...'

'I'm Gatsby' (48)

Nick enters into a conversation with the man at his table who is in the company of a rowdy and nameless little girl. The man is polite and pleasant. He recognises Nick as being from the First Division during the war and reveals that he himself was in the Sixteenth until June 1918. Nick confides that he was sent an invitation by 'this man Gatsby', only to be told that his companion is that man himself! What does the author achieve by allowing the reader (and Nick) to meet Gatsby in person before his identity is disclosed? Does it increase our sympathy for him? Does it give Gatsby a chance to be judged on his own terms without the influence of rumour and innuendo? What are our first impressions of this man? A person of generosity? Bravery? Affability? How does Gatsby's response to Nick's surprise at his identity further define him?

Q   (49) 'He smiled understandingly— ...'

What observations does Nick make about his host's manner of speech?

Q   (49) ' ... I was looking at an elegant young rough-neck ...'

The Chicago call

For the second time in the novel, a telephone call interrupts a conversation. Gatsby takes his polite leave.

Jordan Baker's observations on Gatsby

In a tone of voice that is reminiscent of the earlier disclosure of the gossip that Gatsby is a murderer, Jordan Baker adds more details to the portrait of Gatsby. He once told her that he was an Oxford man, but she does not believe it; he gives large parties.

As if to confirm the latter point, the orchestra starts up with a rendition of 'Vladmir Tostoff's Jazz History of the World'. Gatsby stands apart and aloof.

Q   (51) 'His tanned skin ... I could see nothing sinister ... he was not drinking ...'

His is the only male shoulder that is not touched by a French bob as the girls swoon backward on their partners. Nor does he join the singing quartets. How is such aloofness to be accounted for? Shyness? Reserve? Watchfulness?

Gatsby summons Jordan for a private meeting, and Nick is left alone. This creates a sense of mystery and intrigue; how does this contribute to the atmosphere of the novel and to the character of Gatsby? Do we assume that the meeting is for sexual dalliance? Or do we expect some illegal business arrangement?

NOTE

- the obstetrical conversation being conducted by Jordan's undergraduate partner with two chorus girls
- the young woman who weeps as she sings, and the clownish appearance of her tear-ravaged face as her mascara is caught in her tears
- the fights between so-called husbands and wives
- one woman's anger at a broken promise
- the carrying off of two argumentative wives.

The guests provide images of sadness and disappointment, of lives ravaged by argument and bitterness. Is this Fitzgerald's judgment of his world?

Jordan returns from her half-hour interview, declaring that she has heard the most amazing things. She promises to disclose them further if Nick telephones her at her aunt's house. Nick takes leave of his host as Gatsby is informed of a telephone call from Philadelphia.

The motor vehicle accident

The evening is not yet over. A dozen headlights some 'fifty feet from the door' of Gatsby's house illuminate a violent accident; the car is still upright but shorn of one wheel. The stunned occupant is Owl Eyes, the late patron of Gatsby's library. Even more surprising is his revelation that the driver is still in the car.

Q (55) 'Then, very gradually, part by part, a pale … individual …'

As the crowd departs, Gatsby's house seems surrounded by loneliness.

Q (56) 'A sudden emptiness …'

Nick revises what he has written.

Q (56) 'Reading over what I have written so far …'

He explains that the events he has just narrated took place over several weeks, and during most of that period he worked in the chasms of lower New York in the Probity Trust. He has made friends and has begun to like New York.

NOTE

- Nick's lunches of little pig sausages, mashed potato and coffee with his young colleagues in dark crowded restaurants
- Nick's short affair with a girl who lived in Jersey City (whom he abandoned because of the her brother's animosity)
- his attraction to the 'constant flicker' of people and machines
- his daytime reveries about liaisons with the romantic women of Fifth Avenue
- the poignant loneliness of Nick himself, and of many whom he observes

Q (57) 'Again at eight o'clock … I felt a sinking in my heart …'

- Nick's good wishes to those whose laughter he hears.

Q (58) 'Imagining that I too was hurrying towards gaiety …'

Do Nick's observations of his work life portray the experiences of the common man of the Jazz Age?

Finding Jordan again in midsummer

After losing sight of Jordan Baker, in midsummer Nick finds her again. This time their relationship deepens.

Q (58) 'At first I was flattered … Then it was something more …'

Then she lies about leaving a car outside in the rain with its top down. This incident jogs Nick's memory—she had cheated at her first big golf tournament. He is forced to conclude that 'she was incurably dishonest'(58).

Q (58) 'She wasn't able to endure being at a disadvantage …'

Jordan's motor vehicle accident

Nick dismisses Jordan's dishonesty. He finds himself attracted more to her when they argue about the rottenness of her driving as she passes so close to some workmen that she flicks the button on one man's coat. Why, when he thinks that he loves her, does he keep a brake on their relationship? Is it merely because he feels obliged first to extract himself from the relationship he had back home? Or is it an intuitive rejection by an honest man of a dishonest woman?

Why does the author have the narrator reinforce his personal honesty at this point? Is it because the incidents to be portrayed in the following chapters will demand precise and objective judgment?

Examining the issues

1. Examine the importance of fantasy, violence and deception in this chapter.
2. What are the tensions which emerge from the frivolity of Gatsby's parties?
3. What ghosts and apparitions are encountered in this chapter? Do they do more than foreshadow the deaths of the novel?
4. What contribution does the moonlight make to the atmosphere of Gatsby's parties? Is the rising moon a substitute for the sun, representing the inversion of values in high society of the Jazz Age?

Chapter IV

Sunday morning gossip about Gatsby

The world—or at least glittering society—returns to Gatsby's lawns as the church bells ring out Sunday in the villages along the shore. Do the bells represent a creed which has been abandoned by these visitors?

The conversation centres on Gatsby, whose personal status is enlarged with tales of his bootlegging activities and of the murder which he allegedly committed. His ignominy increases as the speaker imbibes even more of his alcohol—he is 'second cousin to the devil'(60).

A timetable of the grey names of Gatsby's summer visitors

Nick records on the timetable for 5 July 1922 a list of the East's society figures. The names themselves are suggestive; the details Nick ascribes to some of them paint a portrait of a sick and violent society, of people lost in a sea of wealth.

CONSIDER

• the fashionable and often pretentious names

- the moral implications of animal names like Leech, Civet, Beaver, Blackbuck, Hammerhead, Roebuck and Ferret
- the catalogue of suicide, accidental death, adultery, violence, divorce and gambling
- the beatings (Clarence Endive and Etty) and the motor vehicle accident (Mrs Ulysses Swett's automobile ran over Snell's hand when he was very drunk)
- the suggestive reminders of past American achievements and past nobility of its families in the names with historical associations
- the possible reasons for the frequency of Klipspringer's visits
- the vulgarity of humanity suggested in names like Swett, Rot-Gut, the Smirkes, Exckhaust (Exhaust?) and Belcher
- the ever available girls, with flower names or powerful names, and their homogeneity.

A burst of melody from Gatsby's three-noted horn

After attending two of Gatsby's parties, taking a flight in his hydroplane and frequently using his beach, Nick is honoured by a visit from Gatsby himself one morning late in July. Gatsby poses for the occasion.

(62) 'He was balancing himself ...'

What quality seeps through Gatsby's punctiliousness as he does this? Snobbery? Affectation? The desire to create an impression? Restlessness?

The car is Gatsby's status symbol, its impressiveness increased by the labyrinth of windshields and the boxes piled into its interior. Its colours are those of light and the sun.

(63) 'It was a rich cream colour ...'

Nick joins Gatsby for a drive to town, having decided that, despite all the stories bandied around regarding him, he is only the proprietor of what amounts to an elaborate roadhouse next door.

CONSIDER

- the pattern of references to cars and to motor accidents which develops in the novel
- the significance of cars as symbolic statements of their owners' personalities and social status.

Gatsby lets down his guard

The ride provides Gatsby with an opportunity to test Nick's opinion of him. Dropping his guard and a great deal of his pretentious manner, Gatsby embarks upon a narration—'God's truth' (63)—of his past. He says he is the son of wealthy Middle Western people now dead, educated at Oxford in the family tradition.

Why does Nick suspect the veracity of the confidence? Is it Gatsby's sly sideways look? Or the hurried manner in which he referred to Oxford? Or both?

Nick's suspicions about Gatsby are revived.

(64) 'And with this doubt …'

Gatsby nevertheless continues the fantastic story, speaking of his behaviour as a 'young rajah' in the capitals of Europe, collecting jewels (predominantly rubies), painting, and trying to forget 'something very sad that had happened … long ago' (64).

It is only with great difficulty that Nick stops his laughter at the absurdity of it all.

A medal and tales of war and friendship

Then Gatsby's narration becomes unexpectedly serious. He had attempted to die in the war; in doing so, he had led his troops into a heroic action, for which he was promoted to the rank of major. Gatsby produces the medal awarded to him by the people of Little Montenegro as proof of it all. His other souvenir— a photograph from his Oxford days—is equally astounding.

Nick's incredulity is now submerged in fascination.

Nick's imagination is fired by Gatsby's personal revelations. Every rumour and innuendo he has heard is endorsed by his imagination. Gatsby becomes, for him, larger than life.

(65–66) 'I saw the skins of tigers …'

Gatsby reveals his special mission for Nick. Its details will be provided to him by Miss Baker.

'With fenders spread like wings'

The car carrying the two men scatters the light. Is there a retrospective irony when Myrtle is passed by the car that will eventually run her down?

Gatsby uses his influence (a Christmas card from the Police Commissioner) to placate a motorcycle policeman who pulls him up. The city seems to catch the men's ebullient mood as they pass over the Queensboro bridge.

(67) 'Over the great bridge, with the sunlight …'

The hearse

Nick and Gatsby become caught up in a line of funeral cars. Nick is glad that Gatsby's 'splendid car' should become caught up in the sombre procession; is this appropriate?

Lunch in a 'well–fanned' cellar

It is 'roaring noon' as Nick makes rendezvous with Gatsby for lunch. He seems to have intruded upon a private meeting between Gatsby and Mr Wolfshiem.

NOTE

- Wolfshiem's Jewishness
- the sense of subterfuge and cryptic comments about Katspaugh
- Wolfshiem's recollection of the night they shot Rosy Rosenthal in the restaurant across the road at the old Metropole
- the recollection by Nick (assisted by Wolfshiem's accuracy) of the electrocution of the murderers
- the restlessness of Wolfshiem's eyes and the ferocity of his eating
- Gatsby's control of the meeting, but his hasty exit at a remembered appointment
- the history of Wolfshiem's connection with Gatsby (which commenced just after the war)
- Wolfshiem's molar cufflinks, and his claim to fame as the man who 'fixed' the World Series: he is an exemplary cheat, whose dishonesty supersedes even Jordan Baker's
- Wolfshiem's successful evasion of the law.

The lunch concludes with a chance meeting of Gatsby and Tom Buchanan and Gatsby's hasty retreat. What conclusions are to be drawn from Tom's presence at this place?

One October day in 1917 …

That afternoon, in the tea-garden of the Plaza Hotel, Jordan Baker takes up the story of her girlhood meeting in Louisville with the young officer from Camp Taylor, Jay Gatsby. The setting was Daisy Fay's house. By the next year, she had a few beaux herself.

What emotions colour Jordan's first response to Jay Gatsby and to the relationship which he seemed to share with Gatsby? Awe? Envy? A yearning for the same sense of romance?

Q (73) 'The officer looked at Daisy while she was speaking …'

How strong an impression did Gatsby make on her?

NOTE

- Daisy dressed in white and drove a little white roadster to match
- Daisy's popularity with the young officers and the incessant ringing of her telephone
- Jordan's lack of recognition of Gatsby when she met him again on Long Island some four years later

- the rumours that surrounded Daisy, particularly that one winter night she was surprised by her mother packing to go to New York to say goodbye to a soldier, and Daisy's abandonment of soldiers after that
- Daisy's recovery of her gaiety by the next autumn and her debut after the armistice
- Daisy's girlhood home was the most pretentious in the neighbourhood. Does this suggest that Daisy was a princess who lived in a castle? That her background was wealth and pretentiousness? That her family values were firmly rooted in external show?

   (72) 'The largest of the banners …'

What can be made of the brevity of Daisy's 'mourning' for Gatsby? Was she as a young girl (as she is now) fatuous, self-centred and spontaneous, her behaviour motivated by the whim of the moment?

Daisy's wedding to Tom

Jordan recounts the wedding of Tom and Daisy from experience as one of the bridesmaids. She speaks of its pomp and circumstance.

   (74) 'He came down with a hundred people in four private cars …'

The day before the wedding was marred by Daisy's drunkenness and by the tenacity with which she held on to a mysterious letter. Is the letter from Gatsby? It is transformed to 'snow' in the bath: does this tell us that the feelings it evoked were transient? That the emotions it expressed were of little significance in the world of Daisy Fay? That the brief relationship it represented was ephemeral? The next day—her wedding day—all Daisy's reservations about marriage to Tom Buchanan seemed to have disappeared.

Daisy and Tom's honeymoon

The Buchanan marriage commences with a three-month honeymoon in the South Seas. Daisy seems transformed by her love for her new husband.

   (73) 'I saw them in Santa Barbara …'

Is the apparent passion for her new husband surprising, given her doubts about their union the day before the wedding? Is this another sign of her changeability?

Tom's motor vehicle accident

Daisy's marital happiness was short-lived. In late August of their wedding year, Tom's motor vehicle accident on the Ventura road, in the company of one of the chambermaids in the Santa Barbara Hotel, was reported in the newspapers.

The birth of Daisy's child and a year in France

The next April, Daisy gave birth to her daughter. The family went to France for a year before moving back to join the fast set of Chicago. Amongst all the hard-drinking crowd, Daisy refused any dalliance and preserved her reputation.

Daisy was not to hear of Gatsby again until Nick's visit some six weeks before to the Buchanan mansion.

In a victoria in Central Park

Jordan continues her discussion of Gatsby as she drives with Nick through Central Park. She reveals that Gatsby had bought his house in West Egg merely to be directly across the bay from Daisy's house. Gatsby then 'came alive' for Nick. He was a man with purpose, the pursuer of a romantic mission.

> (76) 'He came alive to me ...'

Jordan delivers Gatsby's request: that Nick invite Daisy over to his house one afternoon, letting him come over at the same time. Why is Nick so surprised at the request? Is it because this simple demand for a single opportunity to see Daisy again was the prime motive for Gatsby's purchase of his home and his parties? Or because the plan is directly aimed to facilitate Daisy's viewing of the house? Or because Gatsby had worked so elaborately to ask Jordan to convey his request? Is Nick surprised by the feelings evoked in him for the messenger herself? Or that Daisy is not to know of the extra guest at Nick's afternoon tea?

Examining the issues

1. Examine the mixture of fantasy and truth in Gatsby's narrative of his war experiences.
2. What contribution to Gatsby's history is provided by Jordan Baker's narrative?
3. Images of light and life are at war in this chapter with images of darkness and death. Which set of images triumphs?

Chapter V

Gatsby's house is lit from tower to cellar

Nick is greeted upon his return home by an anxious Gatsby. Why is Gatsby's house lit up? Has he been surveying his rooms in preparation for the anticipated inspection of them by Daisy? Nick rejects Gatsby's offer of a late-night jaunt to Coney Island or a plunge in his pool (which he himself has not used all summer). Nick also rejects the super business deal which Gatsby also offers in payment for the favour. Is this because of the inevitable connection with Wolfshiem which it would bring?

The fateful meeting is to take place 'the day after tomorrow'. Daisy accepts Nick's invitation to come alone.

The day agreed upon pours rain

Gatsby manicures Nick's house for the occasion—even to the point of sending a 'greenhouse' of flowers (and the receptacles to contain it). When he comes over to survey the preparations, Nick cannot help but notice the evidence of sleep-lessness on Gatsby's face. Gatsby appears preoccupied as he settles down to await their visitor.

Just on four o'clock (as Gatsby is ready to abandon the exercise) Daisy arrives, warming the air with the ripple of her voice. Is Nick's description of her voice, as emanating from a throat full of 'grieving beauty' (83), a statement of fact or of romantic supposition on his part? As Gatsby did five years earlier, is Nick falling under the princess's spell?

Daisy sends her chauffeur, Ferdie, away for an hour. Gatsby enters from the rain.

 (83) 'Gatsby, pale as death ...'

NOTE

- the artificiality of Daisy's overheard greeting of Gatsby
- the counterfeit pose adopted by Gatsby at the fireplace, resting his head against the face of the clock on the mantelpiece
- the fall of the clock
- Nick's embarrassment
- the (almost) five-year gap since the last meeting of the former lovers
- Gatsby's desperate revelation in the kitchen that the meeting is a dreadful mistake
- Nick's retreat to the garden and the shelter of a huge black knotted tree
- the recollection of the sad history of Gatsby's house—built by a brewer, then abandoned.

The scene which Nick comes upon on his re-entry into the house amazes him. Both Gatsby and Daisy appear to have been transformed. Their joy at having found each other again is very apparent.

 (86) 'They were sitting at either end of the couch ...'

As they wait for Daisy to wash her tear-stained face, the neighbours applaud the grandeur and beauty of Gatsby's house. Gatsby's explanation of the origins of the money which bought it is confused.

Q (87) 'I was in the drug business ...'

Daisy is taken on a tour of the Gatsby mansion.

CONSIDER

- the pretentiousness and the echoes of Europe in the Marie Antoinette music-rooms and Restoration salons; of the Merton College Library
- the symbolic significance of Gatsby almost toppling down a flight of stairs. Is this an omen of danger?
- the style of Gatsby's bedroom, with its gold toilet set and its wardrobe of shirts and clothes purchased in England
- the significance of Daisy's response to Gatsby's shirts as a revelation of the shallowness and acquisitiveness of her character
- the symbolic shrouding by mist of the green light at the end of Daisy's dock
- Gatsby's control of Ewing Klipspringer, and his awakening him from sleep to play the symbolic 'The Love Nest' on the piano
- Gatsby's changing state of mind.

Q (89) 'After his embarrassment ...'

- the reflection of the excitement inside the house in the excitement which now fills the air outside as the New York commuters make their way home
- Gatsby's declaration of his friendship with Dan Cody.

The episode of the lovers' meeting is orchestrated by Gatsby's home and imagination into a gigantic illusion in which the lovers take on a new intensity of life.

Q (92–3) 'He had thrown himself into it with a creative passion ...'

Confronted privately with the flesh-and-blood Daisy, does Gatsby have anything significant to say? How obvious is his awkwardness with the real woman? Is it only with his gigantic illusion that he feels comfortable?

Nick leaves them to each other.

Examining the issues

1. This chapter is the narrative centre of the novel. Is Nick's tea-party central to the relationship between Daisy and Gatsby?
2. Compare the portrait of Daisy in this chapter with Nick's first vision of her. In the first she is dressed in white, static, posed like an idol. Here she wears lavender and her hair is streaked across her cheek. Do these details suggest a greater vitality in Daisy in her visit to Nick's house? If so, from what is that

extra vitality derived? Is it a reflection of her excited anticipation of the res-
urrection of her feelings for Gatsby?

3. What is the thematic and symbolic significance of the references to clocks in
this chapter? Is Gatsby's encounter with the clock on Nick's mantelpiece
more than a statement of his social awkwardness? Is it also a powerful
reminder that Gatsby, in attempting to reinstate his past relationship with
Daisy, is fighting a (losing) battle against time?

4. Could the interior of Gatsby's house be described as a vulgar mish-mash of
architectural and decorating styles? What might its visual confusion suggest
about Gatsby's confidence in his own social image?

5. How does Gatsby respond to Daisy's reaction to his house? What does his
response reveal about the value that he actually places upon material goods?
Is he defined by this as a romantic rather than a materialist? Does this set him
apart from his society? Or does it suggest a purity of vision that is lacked by
others in his world?

Chapter VI

The notoriety of the man whose real name is James Gatz

Gatsby's notoriety has spread so much during that summer that he has almost
become news himself. A reporter visits his home. Bizarre stories attach themselves to him.

Nick is now privy to intimate personal details of Gatsby's earlier life. His real
name is James Gatz. At seventeen, he had saved Dan Cody's boat from being
broken up and had embarked upon a friendship that was to change his life. His
parents were shiftless and unsuccessful farmers, so he had rejected them and re-
invented himself as the son of God about His Father's business.

   (95) 'He was a son of God ...'

He had worked his way around Lake Superior as a clam-digger and salmon-
fisher, and celebrated his attractive and powerful physicality. He had known
women early and held them in contempt. But his heart was seldom at ease as it
struggled with the fantasies which its owner had created for himself.

   (95) 'Each night he added to the pattern of his fancies ...'

He had worked as a janitor during his brief stay at the small Lutheran
College of St Olaf's. Why was his stay so short? Was it that the college did not

share the grandiose nature of his dreams? He returned to Lake Superior, the place where he was to meet his destiny.

Dan Cody

Cody was fifty years old when the young Jay Gatz rolled up to the glamorous world of his yacht.

NOTE

- Cody was a product of the Nevada silver fields, of the Yukon, and of every mining boom since 1875
- Cody made millions in Montana copper, consolidating his fortune
- he was a magnet to women who tried to separate him from his fortune
- his affair with Ella Kaye was reported in the newspapers in 1902
- Gatsby first used his new name on meeting Cody, and then found himself sailing with the millionaire to the West Indies and the Barbary Coast
- Gatsby became Cosy's confidante and trustee and shared his opulent lifestyle for five years until Cody's rather mysterious death a week after his involvement with Ella Kaye.

Cody brought the savagery, immorality and violence of the frontier to the eastern seaboard. He left Gatsby an inheritance of twenty-five thousand dollars, which Gatsby was not able to claim (Ella Kaye got the millions). He also left Gatsby a substantially filled-out sense of self.

All of this Gatsby told Nick much later, but he narrates the story at this point in his tale of the events of 1922, so as to clear away misconceptions about Gatsby's antecedents built upon wild rumour.

For several weeks after the meeting with Daisy, Nick does not hear from Gatsby. Nick spends his time with Jordan and his energies in trying to ingratiate himself with her senile aunt. Finally, he goes over to Gatsby's house one Sunday afternoon.

A return visit to Gatsby's mansion one Sunday afternoon

Nick is greeted warmly enough by Gatsby, but is surprised at his fellow visitors: Tom Buchanan, a man named Sloane, and a pretty woman in a brown riding-habit.

CONSIDER

- the profound effect upon Gatsby of Tom's presence (it is Tom's first visit to Gatsby's mansion)
- Mr Sloane's refusal of Gatsby's offer of a drink and his deliberate exclusion of himself from the conversation

- Gatsby's acceptance of the woman's dinner invitation, despite having to follow their horses by car and despite Tom's anger

  ℚ (100) "She has a big dinner party and he won't know a soul there ...'

- the trio's abandonment of Gatsby.

Tom and Daisy attend Gatsby's party the following Saturday

Tom has become increasingly concerned that Daisy is running around alone. He attends Gatsby's party with her the following Saturday evening. What is the effect of his presence there? A feeling of oppressiveness? Self-consciousness on Daisy's part? On Gatsby's? Or a sense of sadness? A memorable unpleasantness makes this party stand out from all the others.

  ℚ (100) 'Or perhaps I had merely grown used to it ...'

NOTE

- the roaming of Tom's arrogant eyes
- Gatsby's introduction of Tom Buchanan as 'the polo player'(101)
- the presence of the film celebrity in the company of her director
- Daisy dances with Gatsby
- Gatsby is called yet again to the telephone
- Nick and Daisy sit at a particularly tipsy table
- Nick no longer is amused by Gatsby's parties but rather finds them poisonous and depressing.

CONSIDER

- the ominous discussion of the immersion of the drunken Miss Baedeker's head in Gatsby's swimming pool. Does this create a mood of impending disaster?
- the implications of Daisy's feeling of repugnance at almost all Gatsby's lifestyle and social milieu. Was it the lack of sophistication which appalled her? Or the simplicity which she had no ability or sensitivity to understand?

  ℚ (103) 'She was appalled by West Egg ...'

- Fitzgerald's further reminder of the humble origins of this new consumer society.

Who is this Gatsby anyhow?

Tom's interest in Gatsby is enlivened, and dark. Does he suspect Gatsby's designs on Daisy? Or abhor such a garish display of New Money? Is he disgusted at West Egg's mimicry of East Egg society? Does he distrust the origins of the fortune which sustains his rival? Tom is determined to unravel the mystery that is Gatsby.

What is Daisy's impression of Gatsby's home and of the entertainment which he has provided there? Is she fascinated by the gestures of romance which fill Gatsby's world? Is she offended at the intrusion of Broadway on her world of high society? Is it Daisy's critical view of Gatsby's world that produces the 'something septic' (103) which Nick now notices on the air? Or is it more than this? Has Nick's romantic response to Gatsby and his life been destroyed?

Despite all her criticism of Gatsby's party, Daisy basks in her host's adoration, and in the romance that is totally absent from her own world; perhaps too, she basks in her own superiority above all others in Gatsby's eyes. She tries to catch the limelight by singing accompaniment to the orchestra's 'Three o'clock in the Morning'; is this an attempt to prolong the magical moment when she is the star? Is the song's reference to time also a symbolic reminder that time is running out for the fantasy which Gatsby has constructed?

As the Buchanans leave, Daisy is drawn back to Gatsby's home by the romantic possibilities suggested in the sad little waltz of the year that is being played for the guests who remain. Is her longing look also a reflection of her own fears of losing Gatsby to one of his glamorous guests?

(105) 'Perhaps some unbelievable guest would arrive …'

Do her fears reflect the depth of her feeling for Gatsby? Or her own egotistical delight in Gatsby's obsessive attention?

A request to remain

At Gatsby's request, Nick remains behind until the last guests have gone. Gatsby announces his disappointment at Daisy's response to the entertainment of the evening. He has sensed that she did not like it. Gatsby is unutterably depressed. He wanted Daisy to announce to Tom that she had never loved him, so that they could be married from her house in Louisville, as they might have been five years ago. Daisy refuses to do this. Gatsby cannot understand why the past cannot be repeated.

(106) 'He talked a lot about the past …'

Five years ago, he wanted to suck on the pap of life, to drink in its wonder.

(107) 'Out of the corner of his eye …'

When he and Daisy had kissed, she had been transformed in his eyes to a vision of all the loveliness of the world to which he was forever enslaved.

(107) 'At his lips' touch she blossomed …'

Nick has a faint memory of something in the air like it from his own experience—but the details are lost to him, too, forever.

1. What social boundaries are defined by the events of this chapter?
2. What distinguishes Gatsby's second party, portrayed in this chapter, from the first party that Nick attended (in Chapter III)? Why does he sense a new atmosphere of harshness here?
3. How does the descriptive language of this chapter contribute to the creation of a general feeling of desolation?
4. How does the moon contribute to the sense of a blossoming love between Gatsby and Daisy? Is its accompaniment of their first kiss symbolic of Gatsby's idealisation of the moment?
5. What is the significance of the reference to the ticking of the washstand clock which accompanies Gatsby's construction of his dreams as a young man? Was he even then fighting against time?

Chapter VII

Trimalchio's career is over

One Saturday night, the lights do not go on in Gatsby's house. His career as Trimalchio is over.

When Nick inquires as to his neighbour's health, the door of Gatsby's mansion is slammed in his face by a butler who is unknown to him. He is one of the new brigade of servants employed by Gatsby to replace the old servants who gossiped about Daisy's visits there in the afternoons. Rumour has it that they are not servants at all. Are they also Gatsby's bodyguards? Or his gaolers?

 (109) 'So the whole caravanserai had fallen in ...'

Gatsby's house is no longer a mecca for party-goers. Gatsby transforms it into a castle solely for Daisy.

Gatsby's telephone call

Gatsby telephones Nick to extend Daisy's invitation to him to lunch at her home the following day. Jordan Baker is also to be there. A short time later, Daisy also telephones Nick to repeat the request.

A broiling day—the warmest of that summer

Nick travels to East Egg by train, sharing the heat with his fellow travellers. His commuter ticket is (ominously) stained with the sweat of the ticket man.

At Daisy's house, Jordan and Daisy await the arrival of Nick and Gatsby in a cool, darkened room. What is the impression given by their pose? Goddesses waiting for the adoration of their followers? Cool sophistication in the midst of the strongest heat? Aloofness and insensitivity? Why does the author repeat the set-piece of Chapter I? Is it to demonstrate that these women never change? Or have they? Is it to remind the reader of their demand for the sacrifice of others to the fulfilment of their whims?

Q   (110) 'Daisy and Jordan lay upon an enormous couch ...'

CONSIDER

*   the symbolic deceptiveness of the hiding of Jordan's tan under a film of white powder
*   the gruffness of Tom's voice in the overheard telephone conversation, an argument about his promise to sell a car (he is talking to George Wilson)
*   Daisy's suspicion about the identity of the caller
*   Gatsby's fascination with what he sees, and the sinister foreshadowing of his death by his stance in the centre of the crimson carpet
*   Daisy's overt display of her passion for Gatsby by the kiss stolen in Tom's absence. Is the gesture genuine? Or is it her way of paying Tom back for his dalliance with Myrtle Wilson?
*   Gatsby's surprise at the reality of the child's existence. Does Pammy represent something that cannot be changed about the past? The intimacy of the relationship that Daisy once shared with Nick?
*   Daisy's interaction with her own child. Is there real affection between them? Any true communication?
*   The child's white dress and blond hair. Is she cast in the mould not only of her mother and her 'Aunt Jordan' but also of the blond-headed girls who attended Gatsby's parties?

Tom takes Gatsby on a guided tour. In the heat of the afternoon, the sea beckons both of them. Is the author again reminding the reader of the pioneering past, of the virginal frontier which East Egg once was? Is the sea a symbol of the purity which the land of America has now lost?

Q   (113) 'Ahead lay the scalloped ocean ...'

They all—especially Daisy—struggle against the oppressive heat. Does the heat symbolise the intense passions felt by all present, or the element of lust in these passions? Tom makes subtle reference to his conversion of his garage into a stable; does he intend to remind the other players in the Buchanans' private drama about the Wilsons?

Daisy suggests that they all go to town and then mouths to Gatsby that she loves him. Tom observes the gesture. What is his response? Does it stir his memory of the Daisy he knew five years ago, and the feelings she then felt for

Gatsby? Does it make him angry? He readily takes up Daisy's suggested diversion—perhaps to remove his competitor from his house?

Gatsby reveals to Nick the knowledge that he has acquired about his lover. Her voice is 'full of money' (115). Nick realises that it is this which gave Daisy's voice its special quality.

Tom commandeers Gatsby's car, but Daisy thwarts his plan to take her to town. She accompanies Gatsby in the Buchanans' car. Tom is accompanied by Nick and Jordan, reduced to the position of the chauffeur of two lovers. Does he appreciate the insult? Is this why his subsequent denunciation of Gatsby to his companions is so full of venom?

The gas stop at Wilson's garage

At Jordan's insistence, Tom pulls over at Wilson's garage and demands service from its proprietor. George Wilson informs him that he is sick—and he is indeed green. He informs Tom that he sought Tom's old car—thus the telephone call—because he wants to make some money. He wants to take his wife West—having become aware of her infidelity. Is George's illness at this realisation a symptom of his genuine love for Myrtle?

> (118) 'He had discovered that Myrtle had some sort of life apart from him ...'

Tom's surprise at Myrtle's alleged acquiescence to the plan is reflected in the harshness of his parting words. Yet he is prepared to let George have the car. Why? Is Tom feeling a sense of guilt? Or a new compassion?

CONSIDER

- Tom's position regarding the two women in his life: is he in danger of losing them both?
- Nick's awareness of the parallels between Tom's position and that of George

  > (118) 'I stared at him and then at Tom ...'

- the reminder of the disintegrating moral fabric of Eastern seaboard society provided by the oculist's billboard which oversees the interchange between Tom and the man he has cuckolded
- the mixed emotions which are reflected in Myrtle Wilson's face as she observes the events below—in particular, her jealous terror of Jordan Baker whom she took to be her rival, Tom's wife

  As Tom drives away, he is overcome by panic at the threatened collapse of his personal world.

  > (119) 'There is no confusion like the confusion of a simple mind ...'

He is further disquieted by Jordan's observations about the sensuousness of New York. Is her description of the overripeness of the deserted New York summer afternoons also a comment upon the relationships of all those present on this little excursion? His fear that he will lose his wife and Gatsby forever continues to grow as he loses sight of them in his own blue coupe in the traffic.

The parlour suite of the Plaza Hotel

The party engages the parlour suite of the Plaza Hotel as a cool place in which to imbibe a mint julep. The air is suffocating. An argument between Gatsby and Tom over Tom's criticism of Daisy increases its heat.

Jordan recollects a man called Biloxi, who collapsed in the June heat at Daisy's wedding. Having been carried to the Bakers' house, he remained for three weeks until ordered out by Jordan's father. Mr Baker mysteriously—but, according to Jordan, not suspiciously—died the next day.

CONSIDER

- the symbolic crash of the telephone book
- the symbolism inherent in the sudden explosion into the heat of Mendelssohn's 'Wedding March' from the ballroom below
- Tom's attack on Gatsby's assertion that he went to Oxford.

Tom's final question is addressed singularly to Gatsby: what are his intentions in the Buchanan household? The animosity between them—and the reason for it—is out in the open at last. Gatsby is relieved; Tom is incredulous.

(123) '"I suppose the latest thing is to sit back and let Mr Nobody ..."'

In spite of Daisy's pleas, Gatsby informs Tom that his wife no longer loves him.

(124) '"She's never loved you ..."'

NOTE

- Tom's incredulity
- Gatsby's excitement
- Daisy's confession to having loved Gatsby in secret for five years.

Tom counters Gatsby's assertions with one of his own—he loves Daisy in spite of his sprees. Gatsby demands that Daisy deny ever having loved Tom, and she reluctantly and hesitantly does so. Yet Tom will not abandon his cause. What of the Kapiolani, the Hawaiian park? And the day he carried her from the Punch Bowl in order to keep her shoes dry?

He is triumphant. Daisy cries out that Gatsby wants too much. She loves them both!

Gatsby is utterly defeated. Is this why Tom allows Daisy to leave with him? As a final gesture of power and of control?

- the physical wounding of Gatsby by Tom's words
- Tom's continued savagery upon realising that he has won
- Gatsby's rising panic, which is replaced by an amazing self-control as he defends his position as a bootlegger.

Gatsby's face depicts sinister feelings—more than can be explained by Tom's accusation that he had abandoned Tom's friend, Walter Chase, who had been involved in his business dealings.

(128) 'He looked ... as if he had "killed a man" ...'

Tom's strategy has worked. As Gatsby tries to defend himself against Tom's disclosures, Daisy draws further and further away from him. Her courage has gone.

Nick remembers that it is his thirtieth birthday.

(129) 'Before me stretched the portentous, menacing road ...'

The reassurance of Jordan's hand is barely enough to salvage him from despair at the loneliness of the next decade of his existence. Twilight brings with it a sense of death.

Michaelis is the principal witness at the inquest

The young Greek, Michaelis, who runs the coffee joint beside the ash heaps, is the principal witness at the inquest into Myrtle Wilson's death. The circumstances which led up to it were strange enough in themselves. Wilson, though still ill, had refused to take any time off. Having locked his wife upstairs until the time in two days when they intended to move away, he returned to his pumps. Why is Michaelis surprised at this assertion by Wilson of his independence? Is it that he was usually so dispirited, his wife's man and not his own?

It was after five o'clock when Michaelis withdrew in the face of George Wilson's interrogation about his business activities. A little after seven o'clock, Myrtle, escaping similar viciousness, runs out of the station to her death under the wheels of Gatsby's car.

(131) 'The "death car" as the newspapers called it ...'

Myrtle's left breast is almost torn from her chest. Her mouth is open and ripped at the corners.

Tom, accompanied by Nick, pulls up to survey the accident. The air is full of the wailing of the service station owner, which is joined by the harsh utterance from Tom's own throat as he realises the reason for the commotion.

CONSIDER

- the emotions in the scene of Tom bending over the prone body of his mistress
- the absorption of Wilson in his grief

Q (132) '...Wilson neither heard nor saw ...'

- the negro's identification of the death car as a new, big, yellow car. Is this a symbolic triumph of the black races over the white races about which Tom had spoken?
- Tom's vehement denial of any association with a yellow car apart from driving one that afternoon
- Tom's conviction that it was Gatsby who had run down Myrtle Wilson.

Back at the Buchanans, Tom takes control

Tom arrives at half-past nine and finds Daisy at home. He invites Nick inside, but Nick refuses the invitation. Why? Disgust at the night's events? The birth of a new dislike of Jordan?

As Nick walks down the drive away from the Buchanan house to await his taxi, he is surprised by the emergence of the pink-suited Gatsby from the shadows. Gatsby reveals that it was Daisy who had driven his car into Myrtle. He also explains that he is now waiting to see if Daisy is safe from Tom. She will give a pre-arranged signal by flashing the light of her room, in which she will have locked herself. Nick becomes Gatsby's spy and returns to the house to assess Daisy's situation. The scene he finds confirms the bond between the Buchanans, and Daisy's easy abandonment of the man outside who is so devoted to her. Daisy and Tom are sharing a supper of ale and cold chicken in their mansion's kitchen.

Q (138) 'There was an unmistakable air of natural intimacy about the picture ...'

Nick enters his taxi to leave Gatsby at his sacred vigil—for nothing.

Examining the issues

1. How does the heat of the day contribute to the rising tension in this chapter as Tom guesses the relationship between his wife and Gatsby?
2. Nick refers for the third time in his narrative to the wartime romance of Daisy and Gatsby. How does it differ from the previous accounts?
3. Is the excursion to the Plaza Hotel more than a desperate attempt by the characters to escape from the heat?
4. The golden and silver metallic imagery associated with Daisy is extended in this chapter; how is this done, and by whom?
5. How does the pink suit that Gatsby wears symbolise the reality of his position in society in East and West Egg? Is it a visual reinforcement of Tom's mockery of him as a parvenu, a social upstart? Does it also suggest blood, grimly hinting at the red circle which Gatsby's body will soon make in his own swimming pool?

6. What is the message of the (waning) moon hovering in the western sky? Is this a powerful symbol of the waning of Gatsby's dream?
7. Why is Michaelis's evidence so important in filling in the gaps of Nick's knowledge of the events surrounding Myrtle's death?

Chapter VIII

'Grotesque reality' and 'savage ... dreams'

Does the fog horn with which this chapter begins echo George Wilson's moaning of the former chapter? Is it an appropriate backdrop for the nightmares which trouble Nick's sleep?

Towards dawn, Nick feels an urgency to visit Gatsby. He finds his neighbour overwhelmed by despair or sleep, or perhaps both. A search locates a cigarette for each of them with which to share the morning.

NOTE

*   the sense of emptiness and desertion which engulfs the house
*   the ghostly form of the piano, now silent
*   Gatsby's refusal to leave West Egg in the interests of his own safety, and his clinging to a last shred of hope about Daisy
*   the collapse of Gatsby's fabricated life in the face of Tom's malice.

Talk of Daisy

Gatsby is compelled to speak of Daisy. She was the first 'nice girl' that he had known. She was exciting, and even more desirable because she was desired by so many others. Her house also had its own mystery—every part of it had fascinated him.

(141) 'There was a ripe mystery about it ...'

Was it from Daisy's home that Gatsby derived the inspiration for his own mansion five years later in West Egg?

As a young soldier, Gatsby had known that his time with Daisy was limited. How did he deal with this sense of the impermanency of his happiness? By ravenous exploitation of every minute of his time? By unscrupulousness in his 'taking' of Daisy? By lack of sincerity in his personal behaviour? He saw Daisy as 'extraordinary'. Why did he not realise exactly how extraordinary she really was? What were the consequences of this ignorance for him?

(142) 'He felt married ...'

Two days after their intimacy, he was forever bound to a woman who lived in a world far beyond that of a poor farming boy.

    (142) 'She had caught a cold ...'

The lovers' last afternoon together

During the last afternoon of their month of love, before Gatsby went abroad, he felt closer to Daisy than ever. What was it that made the afternoon so special? The fire in the grate? The flush of her cheeks? Their shared tranquillity? The profound, gentle communication between them?

Gatsby's war experience

Gatsby knew real success in the war. And he knew real despair at the changing tone of Daisy's letters. Was Daisy's despair founded upon the artificiality of her world? Its everchanging face? Its demand for beauty? The sadness of its music?

    (143) 'For Daisy was young ...'

She demanded an immediate direction for her life, and dated dozens of men to find it. Tom Buchanan provided the answer to her restlessness in the middle of spring. She wrote to Gatsby in Oxford about her engagement to him.

Dawn on Long Island

Dawn draws Gatsby back to the present. His world seems imbued, however, with a sense of death.

NOTE

- the tree's shadow
- the ghostly birds
- the promise of a cool day.

Gatsby's gloom

Gatsby continues his narrative. He came back from France while Tom and Daisy were still on their honeymoon and used the last of his army pay to make a pilgrimage to Louisville. The city, because it was her home town, had taken on a special melancholy beauty. He left with a feeling of failure, of not having sought for her hard enough. He had lost the best and the freshest forever.

    (145) 'He stretched out his hand desperately ...'

Nick feels compelled to stay with Gatsby as the morning arrives with its autumn-flavoured air. He misses two trains before he draws away with the promise that he will telephone Gatsby about noon. His parting gift is an acknowledgment of his neighbour's worth.

(146) ' "They're a rotten crowd ..." '

Gatsby expresses a forlorn hope that Daisy will also telephone. He is delighted with Nick's lukewarm corroboration that this might be the case. He is even more delighted by Nick's seizure of the moment to give Gatsby the only compliment he has ever given him. Is this the only moment in the novel when Gatsby does not feel alone? Is it also the author's endorsement of the value of his character?

CONSIDER

• the significance of Nick's acknowledgment of the essential personal worth of Gatsby and its basis in the incorruptibility of his dream
• the symbolism of Gatsby's garish pink suit and the spot of colour which it makes on the white steps of his mansion. Is his murder foreshadowed here? Is there also a suggestion that he is a tainted corrupt man? and society's clown?

(147) '... his face broke into that radiant and understanding smile ...'

Up in the city

Nick is woken at his desk by a telephone call from Jordan Baker, criticising his behaviour to her the night before, but nevertheless demanding to see him. Their conversation ends with the phone being hung up—it does not seem to matter by whom. Nick cannot talk to Jordan across a tea-table that day. Why? Is their relationship at an end? Does her insincerity suddenly disgust him? Is it his anxiety about the man whom her group has excluded?

Nick attempts to telephone Gatsby four times, without success. The operator informs him that the line is being kept open for a call from Detroit. It is just noon.

The events after Myrtle's accident

Catherine had arrived inebriated at the garage and had followed the ambulance bearing her sister's body to Flushing. The crowd eventually dispersed, leaving Wilson to the ministrations of Michaelis.

At about three o'clock, George Wilson emerges from his stupor of grief long enough to focus upon the yellow car that had run down his wife. His memories are painful: Myrtle's return from town with a bruised and swollen face; the expensive dog leash which she had secreted in her drawer. With no friend other than his neighbour and no church, Wilson must deal with these agonies alone. He turns to the god of the billboard.

Four hours after dawn, when Michaelis returns to the garage from his snatched sleep, Wilson has gone. His movements are traced to Port Roosevelt and Gad's Hill. He disappears for three hours, searching the garages for information about the yellow car.

By half-past two, having discovered Gatsby's name, he is in West Egg, at Gatsby's house.

The countdown to Gatsby's death

At two o'clock, Gatsby prepares for the first dip in his pool that summer. The butler waits, on Gatsby's instruction, until four o'clock for the telephone call that does not come. Perhaps Gatsby no longer cares.

> (153) 'If that was true he must have felt that he had lost the old warm world ...'

A rose is now, for Gatsby, a grotesque thing. His dream has died—and with it his world. The ashen, fantastic figure that glides towards him through the trees has come to end a life that is already numb.

One of Wolfshiem's protégés—the chauffeur—hears the shots. The location of Wilson's body a little way off completes the 'holocaust' (154).

Examining the issues

1. What are the nightmare images which dominate Nick's narrative of Gatsby's death?
2. How are Gatsby's last moments of life reconstructed?
3. Is there a beauty in Nick's description of the death scene? What is achieved by this and what judgment of Gatsby does it reflect?

Chapter IX

An endless drill of policemen and photographers

The reports of Gatsby's death are bizarre—and untrue. Catherine silently supports her sister's fidelity to her husband, and this overrides the suspicions that Michaelis's testimony aroused. Gatsby is portrayed as the innocent victim of a man deranged by grief.

Nick takes responsibility for the practical arrangements of Gatsby's funeral. Daisy and Tom cannot be reached by telephone; their intended destination is unknown. Meyer Wolfshiem similarly cannot be contacted. A letter sent by the butler to Wolfshiem is answered by a curt note that offers Gatsby no support at the hour of his death. The only telephone call Nick receives is from a man called

Slagle, complaining about a bogus security deal that has gone horribly wrong for a fellow known only as young Parke.

The third day

After three days, a telegram arrives from Henry C. Gatz from a town in Minnesota. The father acknowledges the son on the third day: is there a religious significance in this? (After all, Gatsby had seen himself as the Son of God.)

NOTE

- the solemnity of Henry Gatz, his sense of helplessness and his dismay
- the statement of poverty in the cheap ulster which Henry wraps around himself against the warmth of the September day
- Henry's affectionate use of the diminutive 'Jimmy' in referring to his son
- the little boys who come to stare and whose presence reminds us of the little boy with hopes and dreams that Gatsby once was
- the awed pride with which Henry's grief is mixed
- the father's endorsement of the worth and lost potential of his son.

> (160) '"If he'd of lived …"'

Klipspringer telephones, but cannot promise Nick that he will attend Gatsby's funeral the next day. He had really called to retrieve a pair of tennis shoes rather than to offer his condolences. Another man whom Nick telephones implies that Gatsby had got what he deserved.

A visit by Nick on the morning of Gatsby's funeral to Wolfshiem's office premises at the Swastika Holding Company is rewarded by Wolfshiem's account of his first meeting with the dead man. In Winebrenner's poolroom at Forty-third Street, he had asked Wolfshiem for a job. They had become the closest of business partners. The necessity to avoid complications means, however, that Wolfshiem will not attend Gatsby's funeral.

> (163) '"When a man gets killed …"'

Does Wolfshiem's comment suggest that murders are commonplace in his world (which was formerly Gatsby's)?

Nick returns to Gatsby's house and to Henry Gatz as it starts to drizzle.

The *Hopalong Cassidy* book

Most precious amongst the father's possessions are a tattered photograph of Gatsby's mansion and the *Hopalong Cassidy* book in which, on the last flyleaf, Gatsby had recorded his timetable for success, dated 12 September 1906.

Nobody comes to accompany Gatsby on his final journey.

A funeral procession of three cars

Gatsby's funeral entourage is small: a motor hearse, then Mr Gatz, Nick and the minister in the limousine, followed by four or five servants and the West Egg postman in Gatsby's station wagon. At the cemetery gates they are joined by the man with owl-eye glasses. It rains heavily.

Daisy sends no message or flower. Gatsby is buried as 'a poor son-of-a-bitch' (166).

A vivid Christmas memory

Nick's memory turns to his visits back West at Christmas time. Why does he remember these times of frozen breath and gloved hands? Is it his subconscious search for a scene of friendship and camaraderie to balance the cold loneliness of Gatsby's funeral, gaiety to counter sombreness? Is the reconstructed scene a romantic and nostalgic vision of a remembered yearning for home? Have Nick's experiences in New York given him a new appreciation of the simple joys and pleasures of his Middle West?

Nick concludes that all of them—Daisy, Tom, Jordan, Gatsby, himself—being Westerners, were unsuited to the life of the Eastern seaboard. Is this conclusion fact or fantasy?

Compared with the happy simplicity of Middle Western life, life in the East is a distortion. Even the moon lacks lustre.

Q (167) 'West Egg, especially, still figures in my more fantastic dreams ...'

How does the scene of the drunken anonymous woman in a white evening dress, borne on a stretcher by four solemn men in dress suits, capture Nick's final feelings about the East? Is this a portrait of decadence? Of the corruption of the American Woman? Of the Mother? Of the submersion of individual identity and dreams in alcoholic stupor?

Such images haunt Nick's consciousness after Gatsby's death.

Q (167) '... the East was haunted ...'

Amidst the signs of winter, Nick decides to go back home. One thing only remains to be done.

A sad farewell to Jordan Baker

Is Nick's farewell to Jordan merely motivated by his desire to 'leave things in order' (168)?

Even on this occasion, Jordan appears posed and false, dressed to play golf and looking like an illustration. She greets Nick's farewell with a surprise of her own—she is engaged to another man. For a moment he doubts his own resolution to leave her behind.

Jordan is critical. Nick had thrown her over on the telephone. What are Nick's feelings as he leaves her? Anger? Hurt pride?

One late October afternoon

One late afternoon, Nick again sees Tom Buchanan. Tom remains alert, aggressive, confident as he strides down Fifth Avenue. His body language is still that of a man who feels the ever-present threat of an invisible enemy. In the dialogue between them arising out of Nick's refusal to shake his hand, Tom reveals the details of George Wilson's missing hours. Wilson had come to the Buchanan household on the day of Gatsby's death. Tom had directed his ire at Gatsby. Why does Tom feel justified in exposing Gatsby to such danger? Is it revenge? The expression of his own grief? Jealousy? Cowardice? Has Tom been duped by his own wife as to the facts of Myrtle's accident? Nick's conclusion about the moral worth of his second cousin and her husband is less than flattering.

    (170) 'They were careless people ...'

What is Nick's implied final judgment of Tom?

The deserted mansion

Gatsby's house now stands deserted; it attracts the interest of a particular taxi driver, who never takes a fare past the gate without stopping. The Gatsby legend lives on—perhaps converted into myth. Does the house take on the atmosphere of a place of pilgrimage? Is it a defaced tomb?

Nick spends Saturday nights in New York. The memories of Gatsby's parties haunt him still. One night he hears a car there and sees its lights shine momentarily on the grand front steps. Is this a lost guest perhaps? Someone who has yet to hear the news of Gatsby's death?

Nick's last night in New York

On his last night in New York, having sold his car to the grocer, Nick undertakes a final pilgrimage to Gatsby's house. What is his motive? Nostalgia? Curiosity? A gesture of respect? What does he find? Anything more than the obscene word scratched by a boy with a piece of a brick on the front step of the house? A moment of quiet reflection against the shadows of surrounding houses and the darkness of the Sound?

As the moon rises over the Sound, the scene is transformed in Nick's imagination to the one which greeted the eyes of the Dutch sailors. The corrupt Jazz Age world is replaced by the 'fresh green breast of the new world' (171).

    (171) 'Its vanished trees ...'

Nick's thoughts return to Gatsby and the wonder which he must have felt as he pursued his dream and felt it within his grasp.

 (171) 'Gatsby believed in the green light ...'

In doing so he represented us all who fight against the current of events and progress which carry all 'ceaselessly into the past' (172).

CONSIDER

- the echo in this final chapter of the first reference to the green light in Chapter I. Has its full meaning now been defined?
- the final link that this last scene establishes between Gatsby and the first settlers of the American continent, who, like him, saw it as a fertile ground for great dreams
- the significance of Nick's final grasp of the universal importance of the dream as a symbol of everything for which people strive, against inevitably over-whelming odds
- the final celebration in the novel of the power of individual imagination.

Examining the issues

1. What contrasts are drawn between Gatsby's position in society at the time of his death and in life?
2. How is Gatsby's personal vision integrated into the continuous flow of American history and the vision which drives it?
3. What is the message of the final symbolic scene of the novel—the voyage of the Dutch sailors and their first vision of the fresh new green world? Is Gatsby's story firmly fixed in this tradition in its belief in the organic nature of life and in the power of hope? Are the dreams of the first pioneers and the subsequent adventurers an anachronism in the reality of Fitzgerald's time? Or do these dreams represent the romantic vision of humanity which always encourages us to swim against the current in order to transform life from a mundane experience? Perhaps swimming against the current, the attempt to overcome all that would destroy one's dreams, is the one true act of heroism of which all humankind is capable.

4

The characters of the novel

The Great Gatsby

Gatsby is an enigma, a character of composite origins, never fully complete in Fitzgerald's mind (as Fitzgerald himself acknowledged).

Gatsby appears to Nick Carraway, the narrator, in the first instance as a kind of vision; he assumes the proportions of a legend, largely through rumour and innuendo, before he comes to Nick as a man, a neighbour wanting a very personal favour, the orchestration of a reunion between himself and his lost love.

Nick states simply at the beginning of the narrative, 'Gatsby represented something for which I have an unaffected scorn.' Despite this, Gatsby's sheer power of personality and his grand gestures transformed him into a 'gorgeous' figure, superior for 'his heightened sensitivity to the promises of life'. Others had lost all sense of romance and of hope. Gatsby retained both, and they gave him a focus in an increasingly restless world. It is these qualities which prompt Nick to vindicate Gatsby before the narrative begins. But these qualities also make him a victim, preyed upon by the selfishness and hedonism and spiritual sterility of his world.

Gatsby's house—a monument to money and bad taste—is Nick's first introduction to him. It is a factual imitation of some Hôtel de Ville in Normandy, a mock institution more comfortable as a public meeting place than as a home. Its history is as coarse as the history of its owner. It is nevertheless a keystone to Gatsby's attempt to rebuild a romance from the past, to recapture the princess who five years before had slipped from his poor grasp into the rich arms of Tom Buchanan. It was for her that he attempted to carve out his share of the heavens and the fortunes which could be made from the crime which was spawned by Prohibition.

Always an outsider, in spite of his entertainment of New York society, Gatsby becomes the subject of gossip and innuendo. Catherine tells Nick that he is a nephew or cousin of Kaiser Wilhelm. Others say that he is a murderer and a German spy, and a bootlegger. He himself describes his experiences (and success) as a soldier, and marvels at his survival when he had tried so hard to die.

Gatsby is a little over thirty; his sophistication is only a veneer. Nick sums him up as 'an elegant young roughneck'. Gatsby's manner of speech, particularly his frequent use of the phrase 'old sport', falls just short of being absurd. His social garishness and ineptitude alienate him from the very persons whose rich manners and easy grace he has set out to emulate.

Mr Vladmir Tostoff plays at his parties. Klipspringer is his boarder; he plays the piano at Gatsby's command but refuses to go to his funeral. Wolfshiem is his business partner and manipulator. They are all enigmatic, shady characters who colour Gatsby's world.

Meeting Daisy again at Nick's house, Gatsby is 'consumed with wonder at her presence'. Around her he constructs an illusion of colossal vitality—but it is doomed to founder upon the hard rocks of reality. His princess is a corrupted maiden, repelled by the simplicity and vulgarity of Gatsby's life and wealth. Once he realises this, the whole construction of his life collapses; his career as Trimalchio (the vulgar social upstart) is over.

Why and how did 'the dead dream slip away'? Gatsby followed a holy grail. His life is transformed into a quest for it. When it is stolen by his rival (for the second time) he no longer has any reason for living. His solitary death under the dark moon is a nightmarish anticlimax to the grand romantic gesture which has been his life.

Tom Buchanan

Tom Buchanan is a physically powerful man, used to getting his own way and more than a match for an 'upstart' like Gatsby. He is introduced in a set piece, standing on his front steps as master of all that he surveys. His stance is at the same time aggressive and defensive. His clothes are symbols of his masculine power and of the physical force—even brutality—with which he is prepared to protect his possessions. The impression which he gives is that of a Fascist stormtrooper serving in a silent revolution (which Hitler was to make real in the next decade).

Despite Gatsby's attempts to claim his wife from him, to reverse the choice she had made in the past, Tom's position of dominance falters only momentarily—in the heat of the day on which he and his rival accompany Daisy, Jordan and Nick to the Plaza Hotel. The events which follow the destruction of Gatsby's hope there see Tom restored to full control.

Aggression is Tom's key characteristic. Sturdy and 'straw-haired', he is a little younger than Gatsby at 'about thirty', with a hard mouth and a patronising manner. His body is cruel and strong, and the muscles which ripple across his shoulders are often put to use by their owner in muscling his guests, bruising the knuckles of his wife, or smashing his mistress's nose. Tom Buchanan is, as his wife says, 'a brute of a man'.

Tom is self-indulgent and disloyal in his marriage, passing from one woman to the next in an endless expression of his manhood. His full motivation is difficult to fathom, however, as he seeks philosophic answers to the decay of civilisation in books full of second-hand and outmoded ideas. He lack the self-perception or critical awareness to realise that it is the behaviour of men like himself and their hedonism which lies at the root of the decay.

Daisy Buchanan (née Fay)

Daisy Buchanan is the caged princess, enveloped in a world of glamour and money. She would not dream of departing from this world, to the acquisition of which she has sacrificed every moral virtue of her being, including that of motherhood. Her lack of moral and personal substance is embodied in her form, in her dress and, most of all, in her voice. It is an 'indiscreet voice', the voice of the 'golden girl', a 'king's daughter' living 'high in the white palace'.

The lines by D'Invilliers, the epigraph of the book, introduce the reader to the shallowness of Daisy and at the same time to her attractiveness. She makes demands on all those around her in her careless pursuit of ever more elaborate means of self-indulgence.

Nick's first vision of Daisy is as a doll, an idol, deliberately and artificially arranged, and 'buoyed up as though ... upon an anchored balloon'. Both she and Jordan Baker are ironically dressed in virginal white, giving all the appearance of moths of fairies who had just landed after fluttering around the house. The symbolic suggestion is heavy and condemnatory. Beautiful and fairylike as this woman is, she, like her friend Jordan, is entirely without moral substance.

She has an 'absurd charming little laugh' which accompanies the most meaningless platitudes: 'I'm p-paralysed with happiness.'

She has a 'way' which makes you feel (self-deceivingly, of course) that 'there [is] no one in the world she so much wanted to see'. Under this external confidence, however, are 'turbulent emotions'. With the whole world at her feet and the means to enjoy it, she is nevertheless lost, 'pretty cynical about everything'. Courted by Tom's wealth, she became a member of a world in which marriages were to be arranged, and partners bought. She is not capable of responding to love—the pure love of Gatsby.

Jordan Baker

Miss Baker's fluttering lips symbolise the dishonesty that is her essence. These, together with an 'exhibition of complete self-sufficiency', make her lethal in dealing with the emotions of others, including Nick Carraway. Yet, unsavoury as she is as a human being, her moral inadequacies and her lack of sentiment and sincerity are hidden beneath a facade that is extraordinarily attractive:

[Her] low thrilling voice ... was the kind of voice that the ear follows up and down ... her face was sad and lovely with bright things in it, bright eyes and a bright passionate mouth, but there was an excitement in her voice that men who had cared for her found difficult to forget: a singing compulsion, a whispered 'Listen', a promise that she had done gay, exciting things just a while since and that there were gay, exciting things hovering in the next hour …

She is a 'slender, small-breasted' girl. Her cadet-like posture, however, links her with the military image of Tom Buchanan and the Fascist cruelty that is the basis of his (and her) moral code.

She is a bored young woman, given to stating yawningly that there is something that she ought to plan; but she has no real intention of making any plans at all except for her own comfort.

Aimless but attractive, Jordan Baker immediately attracts Nick. Telling him that he reminds her of a rose (the perfect symbol of love), Jordan exudes a 'stirring warmth … as if her heart was trying to come to you'.

Jordan is a cheat, and yet controlled by the demands of her own jaunty body. Her face dissembles for her, and hides the scandal attached to her cheating both at golf and at life.

Myrtle Wilson

Myrtle Wilson is Fitzgerald's representative of the working woman. She aspires to live out her own American Dream by escaping the confines of poverty and the spiritlessness of her class. She creates for herself a model—albeit a poor model—of the rich upper-class world inhabited by Daisy Buchanan and Jordan Baker and women like them. Who could blame her from seeking an escape from 'the grey land and the spasms of bleak dust which drift endlessly over it'? What attraction could 'the blond, spiritless man' that was her husband possibly have?

It is ironic that the woman who seeks to be somebody is introduced in the novel by her rival (and role model) Daisy Buchanan as 'some woman in New York'. And she is, indeed, some woman. The first description of her by Nick recognises the voluptuousness that underlies the poverty of her situation. She is, it seems, a woman of substance in comparison with the faerie-like, ethereal quality of Daisy, the Jazz Age sophisticate. Her figure is not waif-like like Daisy's, but 'thickish' and 'faintly stout'. A woman in her 'middle thirties', she has already passed the first blush of youth to achieve a mature presence. She is not beautiful—but vital, alive, 'as if the nerves in her body were continually smouldering'. This is her restlessness.

Tom treats her with disdain. His acquaintances, we are told, 'resented the fact that he turned up in popular cafés with her, and leaving her at a table, sauntered about, chatting with whomsoever he knew'.

Childless, Myrtle compensates her maternal longing with the purchase of a lapdog: 'They're nice to have, a dog.' In doing so, she provides an ironic parallel to Daisy's attitude to Pammy. Both are creatures to be brought out and petted and then put away.

Nick Carraway

Nick Carraway returns from World War I a restless and ambitious young man. He is determined to grasp the opportunities for success and wealth that New York offers. He fancies himself another Midas, Morgan and Maecenas.

The reality of New York proves less favourable to his advancement than he had hoped. Life as a bond salesman leads only to the ranks of workers who know real loneliness in the darkened streets and to a humble cottage clinging to the edge of the less fashionable of the two Eggs.

The only advantage which Nick has over other newcomers is his connection to Daisy Fay (a distant relative) and her husband, Tom Buchanan (a friend from his days at Yale). Fate makes him the neighbour of the greatest parvenu of them all—Jay Gatsby.

Nick is excited by New York at first, especially by the glamour and extravagance of his neighbour's parties. Nick has an initial tolerance and passivity which cause the other characters to confide in him. They sweep him into their own lives and illicit activities.

He rejects Gatsby's bribe of an opportunity to make a lot of money in some shady business deal, but he is sufficiently free-thinking to engage in a minor flirtation with a girl at his office and a major flirtation with the dishonest Jordan Baker. He is saved from serious damage as a result of the latter by a sense of doing the right thing and a need to preserve the order of things by dealing first with the relationship which lingers back home. Nick survives emotionally because he keeps a certain distance from people and events.

Nick's emotions are finally trapped, however by his affection, regard and sympathy for Gatsby. They have much in common: both Middle Western boys who are pioneers in a New World. Gatsby differs only in having more immediate success—a result of his willingness to engage in illegal activities. Gatsby's pursuit of wealth is motivated by a commitment to a vision of womanhood in Daisy which transcends wealth and the corruption which it brings. Both men are, and remain, outsiders.

Once Gatsby is dead, Nick takes responsibility for arranging the funeral and finalising his affairs. This places Nick in the centre of events that demonstrate the true emptiness of the New World which he has sought, and the indifference to all decent values of its inhabitants, the Buchanans amongst them. For this, Nick pays a price. He is overcome by bitterness and retreats home. He refuses to succumb to the power of wealth, or to capitulate to the evil which rules the world of the East which is built upon it.

George Wilson

Denounced by his wife Myrtle as 'unfit to lick her shoe' (37), George Wilson belongs to the new underclass of dispirited men who eke out a living servicing

the needs of the rich, while clinging to inevitably doomed dreams of obtaining, through their efforts, wealth and happiness of their own.

George is a garage owner and would-be car dealer living on the promise of a special deal from the man who has made his wife his mistress. His lack of success to date is symbolised by the dust-covered wreck of a Ford which cowers in the corner of his garage. Perhaps its timidity is also his, for he is a servile man who lacks spirit until fate calls him to avenge the murder of his faithless wife. Like Gatsby he too has fixed at the centre of his dream a corrupt woman whose affections are attracted by a man wealthier than himself. Once handsome and now hanging desperately to a 'dim glimmer of hope' (28), he is the other side of the coin to Gatsby's success. Completely broken (like Gatsby) at the destruction of his dream with the final loss of the object of his affections, his final steps are those of a husk of a man, already rendered a ghost by his sense of grief and loss.

George Wilson's final act is based upon a misconception as to the true identity of the murderer of his wife—a self-deception deliberately fostered by Tom Buchanan. He is a victim to the end, a tool of Tom's revenge against the man who would steal his wife. The rag-doll image, in which Tom holds George upright to steel him for his final moment, symbolises George's powerlessness, his abandonment of proper judgment, and his loss of substance in a society which exploits the weak and then abandons them.

Lucille and Chester McKee

The McKees reside in the apartment directly beneath Myrtle and Tom's at 158th Street. Better-off than the Wilsons, they represent a middle class in New York society, people who have avoided the extreme poverty of the wasteland of the Valley of the Ashes, but are excluded from the lifestyle of the wealthy.

The McKees are a desperate pair, a two-person business enterprise seeking to market the husband's obviously limited photographic skill by cashing in on the egotism of their clients. He is 'pale' and 'feminine' (32), a man manipulated by his shrill-voiced wife. She declares only too readily how close she came to marrying someone who was below her—a fate which parallels Daisy Buchanan's choice and which her friend Myrtle did not avoid.

Despised by Tom Buchanan as inconsequential but necessary background to Myrtle's parties, the McKees nevertheless provide him with an opportunity to impress and to parallel, in a mean-spirited way, Gatsby's generosity to his guests. The cost is small—a plate of sandwiches and a couple of bottles of whisky. To-gether they represent the ugliness of the new consumerism gripping their world.

Catherine

Myrtle's sister Catherine, a slender, worldly party-girl of dubious morals, symbol-ises the corruption of young womanhood in Gatsby's world. She is the individual face given by Fitzgerald to Gatsby's female party-goers, a restless young woman who purveys the gossip derived from her attendance at his mansion. She tells Nick she is fearful of Gatsby, that 'they say he's a nephew or a cousin of Kaiser Wilhelm's' (35), a man who is as threatening as he is generous. She is equally forthcoming—if equally ill-informed—in her gossip about Tom Buchanan and his wife and the supposed reason for Tom's not seeking a divorce.

She is aligned perhaps to Meyer Wolfshiem by the pottery bracelets that adorn her arms (his wrists sport human molars). It is the values of his world, after all, that she has espoused. Her lack of personal substance is reflected in her itinerant lifestyle and symbolised by the blurred effect which her natural eyebrows, in struggling to reassert themselves, give to her powdery white face. She is a social butterfly and garish social clown.

Meyer Wolfshiem

Wolfshiem represents the corrupt core of the novel. The character is based on a New York gambler, Arnold Rothstein, who was gunned down in 1919. He is both physically and morally repugnant.

Wolfshiem's name represents his carnivorous business and social habits as he preys on humanity in order to serve his own material ends. He is a man, as Nick Carraway realises at the end of the novel, prepared to 'play with the faith of fifty million people—with the singlemindedness of a burglar blowing a safe'.
Wolfshiem is part of the dust that blighted Gatsby's dreams, a powerful man who at fifty years of age exists at the heart of the corruption of Jazz Age America. He met and 'saved' the vulnerable Gatsby from poverty and hunger just after the war, but introduced him to a web of crime which engulfed him just a surely as George Wilson murdered him.

Wolfshiem inhabits the underworld of New York society and is its 'denizen' (71), a man who, as Gatsby proudly explains, 'fixed the World Series back in 1919 (and got away with it)'. A 'small, flat-nosed Jew' (68), with an exceptionally large head adorned by luxuriant nostril hair, his personal history is even more shady. It includes being present at the Metropole when his friend Rosy Rosenthal was shot at four o'clock in the morning, and using standover tactics against those who refuse to co-operate with his plans.

Wolfshiem is a man of 'business gonnegtion[s]' (69), whose offer to Nick of a business deal is turned down in spite of all the wealth it promises. Nick concludes that it is his business dealings which explain Wolfshiem's restlessness and his readiness for attack.

Like Tom Buchanan, Wolfshiem is an arch-manipulator—and very skilful at it. He significantly dissociates himself from Gatsby after the latter's murder, preferring to remain in the shadows, and failing this last test of loyalty to a faithful protégé.

Wolfshiem's moral ugliness and personal ruthlessness are symbolised by the cufflinks that adorn his wrists: fine specimens of human molars.

5

Examination and essay topics

1. Scott Fitzgerald's women are powerful expressions of a new age. Discuss in relation to *The Great Gatsby*.

Checklist

Here are some facts, themes and opinions to consider as you review the female characters:

- Fitzgerald's intimate knowledge of and interest in talented, attractive, adventurous and self-indulgent people
- Fitzgerald's fascination with power and social elitism
- the treatment in the novel of marital fidelity and breakdown, of husband–wife relationships
- the novel's treatment of dishonesty and corruption, and the active part which women play in this as well as their inspiration of it
- the fervent desire of the female (and male) characters to be loved
- the stereotype of the Roaring Twenties woman—fragility and no substance
- sensuality and seriousness
- the portrayal of motherhood
- the power of dreams and of illusions
- women as barometers of the health of society: consider Daisy Buchanan, Jordan Baker, Myrtle Wilson, Catherine, the female party guests, the romantic pedestrians of Fifth Avenue, including the drunken woman in the white evening dress
- the numbers of emancipated young women who flock to Gatsby's parties, including Lucille, Jordan's friend, as well as the sexual freedoms enjoyed in the novel by Jordan Baker, Myrtle Wilson and (with Gatsby) Daisy Buchanan. Note Nick's hostility to the New Women who was born in postwar American society.
- however emancipated they are, the women in the novel depend on men: they are brought to the parties, fall back into men's arms, lay their heads upon men's shoulders; they are are locked in their rooms, beaten, and trapped by men in sad marriages. Even the most emancipated—Jordan Baker—capitulates to marriage.

2. How does the setting of *The Great Gatsby* contribute to its meaning?

The narrative begins in the spring of 1922. From this point it develops its characters and its themes against a background of vividly individualised settings which are heavily and intriguingly symbolic.

Checklist

The West

Nick Carraway, the narrator, is an emissary to the East from the West, a graduate of New Haven. As a result of the war, he came to believe that the environment of his childhood—the West—was 'the ragged edge of the world'. His experience of the East forces Nick to re-evaluate the old frontier and to seek the safety of its secure towns and simple lifestyles.

World War I

The ravages of World War I dwell just below the surface of consciousness in several of the characters. The war was the catalyst in forcing Gatsby to abandon Daisy. It lives on in Nick Caraway's memory, and it continues to inform his life as he is overcome by a restlessness to find in peacetime the excitement of the battlefield.

The East

'A pair of enormous eggs, separated only by a courtesy bay, jut out … like the egg in the Columbus story, they are both crushed flat at the contact end … dissimilar … in every particular except shape and size' (10). The contrast between these two communities and, more importantly, the gulf between them is stressed from the beginning of the novel. The two microcosmic worlds they embody are governed by Tom Buchanan and Jay Gatsby respectively. The former rules over the riches of the the Establishment, the world of Old Money, built historically upon corruption and exploitation but far enough removed from it not to feel tainted. The New Money founds the world of Gatsby. It is a world of aspiration and dreams built on corruption that is always close to the surface, and displays itself with éclat at the parties held by its ruler. This world is crass, yet attractive in the rawness of its emotions and the honesty of its vulgarity. It is the place of pilgrimage for the residents of East Egg, who are in search of the vitality that their riches have submerged. Both worlds are joined in their abandonment of a moral code. They are both damaged eggs. They are the ultimately damaged genitalia of America—the seed source of the new ideas that are to inform its civilisation, the procreation of which is threatened by the floating dust of the wasteland's sterility.

East Egg

East Egg housed the Establishment, the Old Money families represented by the Buchanans. It 'glittered' and allowed Nick Carraway an entrée based upon his familial connection with Daisy, his 'second cousin twice removed'. This is the milieu of the 'enormously wealthy', yet it admits people like Nick, who had migrated East from Chicago 'in a fashion that took your breath away'. In New York, the Buchanans and people like them 'drifted here and there unrestfully wherever people played polo and were rich together' (11). The facade of the Buchanans' home symbolises their entrenched position and the solidity and status of their wealth. It has no rawness. Its lawn is a quarter of a mile in extent, and runs right up to bright vines that are in harmony with the 'reflected gold' of the French windows—a veritable North American Palace of Versailles. The symbols suggest the palace of King Midas, and a corrupt Garden of Eden. Are Tom and Daisy the corrupt Adam and Eve who have constructed their own morally corrupt Paradise?

West Egg

West Egg is the less fashionable of the two Eggs. It owes its wealth to the *nouveau riche*, men like Gatsby, who have adopted the trappings of wealthy culture but remain more or less isolated from it and shunned by its members. Gatsby's newness to the rich social milieu to which he aspires is symbolised by the newness of his house. A glamorous yet gauche building, it has all the accoutrements—such as a swimming pool and forty acres of lawn—yet has an atmosphere of raw vulgarity: a 'thin beard of ivy'. Its inhabitant was a criminal, a bootlegger, a mystery and a gentleman. It had been built by a brewer and had a tragic past. West Egg had room for the 'small eyesore' which was Nick Carraway's house, whereas East Egg housed only the superlatively wealthy. Daisy's view of West Egg was less than complimentary:

> She was appalled by West Egg, this unprecedented 'place' that Broadway had begotten upon a Long Island fishing village—appalled by its raw vigour that chafed under the old euphemisms and by the too obtrusive fate that herded its inhabitants along a short cut to nothing. She saw something awful, in the very simplicity she failed to understand (103).

West Egg defines people by their reaction to its vulgarity and shamelessness. The final portrait provided of it and of the East is of a place that is deadened by winter, abandoned by its people and in the last stages of real decay.

The effects of the war

Nick's migration to the East in search of a career in the bond business is his answer to the 'restlessness' that he feels as a reaction to the effects of the Great War. His restlessness is symbolic of the emotional and psychological restlessness of the nation. Nick escapes from the memory of global conflict to enter a society which has its own pariah: Tom Buchanan, a man proud of his Aryan 'Nordic' background, and 'nibbling at the edge of stale ideas'. Nick comes to a new frontier and a new battle—to establish himself as an individual in a world in which individual integrity has long been surpassed by individual wealth. Demobbed from one army, he is tempted to become a recruit in a new army—an army of selfish service rather than of selfless sacrifice. His would-be recruiter is Jordan Baker—a cadet in uniform at their first meeting. The war to be fought in 1922, despite its different ethics, was in many ways a re-run of the war fought in the previous decade: a battle between tradition and conservative values of loyalty and honesty of the Old Order on the one hand, and a New Order based on cruelty and hedonism. In the world of the novel, however, victory belongs to the New Order. This is a reversal of the outcome of the global conflict of World War I. Gossip has it that Gatsby 'was a German spy during the war' (45). The truth of this is never established, but Gatsby himself outlines his own involvement in the war (49). His revelations amount to a confession—extraordinary, in the context of the novel and of Gatsby's own life, for its candour. For once, Gatsby lets down his guard. Meyer Wolfshiem tells Nick the details of Gatsby's experiences after his return from the war with his chest full of medals. It is not a happy picture.

The Valley of Ashes

The Valley of Ashes by its name provides the novel with a biblical perspective—it is a place of repentance, of suffering and of punishment. It embodies the spiritual sterility of the society of which it is a central part, embodied in the corruption of biblical symbols of fertility such as wheat and water. Its harvest is bitter. This is a bleak land, an ash heap of dreams and of disappointed lives, a solemn dumping-ground presided over by a disembodied god—the eyes of Doctor T. J. Eckleburg—a god who is sightless and indifferent to the sufferings of his world. The 'foul river' is part of this hell. It is a corruption of the classical symbol of the River of Life. The small settlement of the wasteland is a community in an advanced stage of decay. Its garage is 'unprosperous and bare', owned by an 'anaemic spiritless man'.

The apartment

The love-nest of Myrtle and Tom is a small slice of Versailles in 'a long [ironically] white cake of apartment houses' whose shape is itself a bitter parody of the wedding cakes of white weddings. On 158th Street in New York, it has the trappings of luxury and its own social set: the McKees and Catherine, Myrtle's sister, dreadful parodies of the more sophisticated guests who attend the parties of East Egg. Their own soirées are microcosms of the larger gatherings sharing in their pretensions and their violence.

The parties—the Land of Romance

Gatsby's parties are his bait to catch a moth—Daisy Buchanan. They symbolise the conspicuous consumption of the Jazz Age, the shallowness of its human interaction. The mountain of pulpless halves of fruit that they produce is a symbol of the shallowness and conspicuous consumption of the social set which they entertain. The parties are frequented by 'swirls and eddies' of people whom neither Gatsby nor Nick know, including two girls in identical yellow, the 'stage twins'. At these parties, as at Myrtle's apartment, violence and adultery form the code of social behaviour. Nick Caraway is encouraged by the consumption of two bowls of champagne to suspend his judgment of the participants. 'The scene had changed before my eyes into something significant, elemental, profound' (48).

The Frontier

Jay Gatsby evolved into the Great Gatsby upon a foundation of character built upon the experiences of the Western frontier. This background is set out for the reader on page 95 at the beginning of Chapter VI. Refer to it. Note the physical reality of clam digger and salmon farmer, the simple goodness perhaps of a life lived in touch with Nature.

The Plaza Hotel, New York

This hotel (Chapter VII, 120) is the scene of the last great party of the novel— the confrontation between Daisy, Tom and Gatsby in the presence of Nick and Jordan. Consider the details of the place carefully. It is here that Gatsby's dream is finally destroyed. Tom saw it as the 'last barrier of civilisation'. Why?

The cemetery—The funeral of Gatsby

> …our procession of three cars reached the cemetery and stopped in a thick drizzle beside the gate—first a motor hearse, horribly black and wet, then Mr Gatz and the minister and me in the limousine, and a little later four or five servants and the postman from West Egg, in Gatsby's station wagon … it was the man with the owl glasses (165).

3. 'The Great Gatsby portrays the death of the American Dream.' Discuss.
   This statement focuses upon the representative nature of the biographies in the novel—in particular, Gatsby's life and Nick Carraway's experiences in 1922. The American Dream was to establish a New World, in which everyone by hard work could find wealth and happiness in an egalitarian society, free of the repressions and hatreds and divisions of the Old World.

   The conclusion of the novel is set in December, with 'winter snow … murky yellow cars … dim lights'. Nick Caraway returns to the Middle West in an atmosphere of unreal sadness and loss. The glitz of the East is empty and decaying; it has lost all its attraction and promise for the young soldier who had come to partake of its glory and share in its promises of success. The destruction of his hope, the process by which he abandons his optimistic vision for postwar America, is the emotional and narrative framework of the novel. His loss is also America's.

The last pages of the novel evoke a historical memory of a clean fresh land, a land thought to be suitable for the stuff of dreams. The dream is embodied in stream imagery. Note how the current of the past was vigorous, the water clean. Compare this with the sterility and the lethargy of the river that runs through the Valley of Ashes. What is the final message here? That the American Dream was flawed from the beginning? That the American Dream is a hopeless imaginative excursion into the realms of romanticism and fairy-tale? That the American Dream is a magnificent ideal, but has been corrupted by its means and its own success and become a celebration of hedonism even more corrupt and corrupting than the old values left behind?

Checklist
* analyse the juxtaposition of water (with which the American Dream is associated), a symbol of hope and of fertility and spiritual revival with dust, the symbol of spiritual sterility and defeat
* analyse the juxtaposition in the novel of green and gold (and silver); the one representing innocence and faith; the other representing corrupt experience and wealth
* consider the importance in the novel of the references to the colour white. For Daisy and Jordan and Gatsby's party-goers, it is the colour of lethargy and inaction—a symbol of moral, spiritual and emotional emptiness. The colour of moths, it represents insubstantiality, the lack of focus and commitment which underlies the restlessness of the rich. It contrasts starkly with the pink and yellow suits worn by Gatsby.

4. What is the role of Nick Carraway in *The Great Gatsby*?
   Nick Carraway is at the same time a device and a character; he observes and narrates the action of the novel, and also participates. Any discussion of his contribution in the novel should consider the following.

Checklist
* the journey of discovery on which Nick embarks as he leaves the security of his Middle Western home to pursue wealth and status in the East. His experiences there are his initiation, a rite of passage, into a racier, more hedonistic and glamorous world. The discovery that he makes as a result is that, despite its colour and overt magnificence, life in the East brings none of the satisfactions and joys of life in the West.

- Nick's representation of the restlessness that gripped his generation (both men and women) after the horrible debacle of World War I.
- Nick's role as observer and judge of the events of 1922, and the special perspectives which he provides of Gatsby.
- Nick as participant in, and facilitator of, the action (especially in his orchestration of the meeting of Daisy and Gatsby, and in his organisation of Gatsby's funeral).
- Nick as the vehicle of the author's final judgment on the society which he has created.

5. Who is this enigma known as Gatsby?

6. How justified is the title of the novel, *The Great Gatsby*?

Many examination questions focus on the figure of Gatsby. He is, after all, the novel's most complex character, and the novel is named for him. He is its central focus, its most fascinating human being, and its most powerful symbol. The novel is really the story of the events over a year which led to his murder. His death is the symbol of the death of the Dream that lies at the heart of American consciousness.

Checklist

An outsider

Gatsby is a parvenu (newcomer, upstart), a man desperate to be part of the High Society of the East but excluded and excluding himself from it: note the powerful image of a man pursuing a private quest in the first set piece of Chapter I. Gatsby preserves his integrity even at his own parties: none of the girls present swoon into his arms; no French bob touches his shoulder. He maintains a lonely and pointless vigil outside Daisy's house after Myrtle is run down. Discuss the significance of Gatsby's lonely pilgrimage to Daisy's house in Louisville after the war; Gatsby standing isolated in his pink suit on his front steps as he is abandoned by the world; Gatsby's aloneness at the time of his death; and his virtual abandonment by all at his funeral. Are these isolationist moments of Gatsby's at the same time a condemnation of society and an acclamation of Gatsby's moral and emotional superiority to it?

A mysterious and exotic figure

Images of Gatsby are created through gossip and innuendo—he is said to have been a spy and to have killed a man; he is alleged to be the Kaiser's nephew. He fabricates his own history, yet his real story is just as amazing; he is a war hero and an active member of a criminal syndicate. He is a romantic and a dreamer, yet he has transformed himself into a millionaire in less

72

than five years. He scares some of his party-goers, yet he has the sincerest and easiest of smiles. Nick disapproves of him, yet he is inexorably drawn to him.

From poverty to riches

Gatsby has risen from poverty to great wealth. He has moved from a torn jersey and canvas pants to a whole wardrobe of suits: a white suit worn with a silver shirt and gold-tipped tie; a yellow suit that matches the colour of his automobile; and a pink suit, luminous under the moon as he takes what is to be his last farewell of Nick. Gatsby's car is huge and glitters with glass and nickel—Nick calls it a 'circus wagon' (115), but it becomes a 'death car'. Gatsby's enormous house is a grotesque exercise in bad taste, yet he turns it into a light-filled fairy palace for Daisy.

A dreamer

Gatsby is a dreamer who builds his future on the hope of repeating the past. He devotes his life to the accumulation of great wealth, which he believes will put him in a position to win Daisy, a woman who was transformed by their first kiss into his princess. His life becomes a quest for her; he reconstructs his persona so that he might pursue her—but he is rewarded only by her disgust and betrayal. As a real woman, she is unable to live up to the ideal vision which his imagination had constructed of her.

A victim

Gatsby is also a victim. He is preyed upon by the vulgarity and the violence of which he has become a part in order to gain wealth, following Dan Cody's example, to win his girl. He is preyed upon by the 'foul dust' of the New World, the hedonism, self-centredness and restlessness of a society which has no patience with a man's faithful commitment to a romantic vision. He breaks up 'like glass against Tom's hard malice'.

7. 'The Great Gatsby is a portrait of a corrupt society. It is peopled by bootleggers and speakeasies, corrupt police and judiciary, the depressed and the suicidal, adulterers and deviants, cheats and bullies. Its main events are arguments, accidents and assassinations.' Examine the novel from this point of view.

8. 'The Great Gatsby dissects the causes of the complete breakdown of American morals and manners.' Discuss.

   The important thing to remember about these statements is their breadth. They require you to adopt an expansive approach to your discussion. The first statement provides clear headings under which you should analyse the novel. A successful answer to questions like these must be based on a detailed knowledge of the novel, both its characters and events.

Checklist

The bootleggers, the fixers and the gamblers
- Wolfshiem, the man who fixed the World Series and was organising the Katspaugh deal

Gatsby
- the new 'servants' who take over Gatsby's house
- Gatsby's associates in Chicago and Philadelphia who continually telephone his house
- Gatsby's chauffeur, one of Wolfshiem's protégés

The speakeasies
- Gatsby's house is an Hôtel de Ville—one gigantic speakeasy for the whole of West Egg, East Egg, New York and Broadway society while the parties last
- the saloons lining the cobbled slum passed on the way to the Valley of Ashes
- the Forty-second Street cellar restaurant serving highballs to customers like Gatsby and Wolfshiem

Corrupt police and officials
- Gatsby's close 'friendship' with the Police Commissioner
- the traffic policeman who lets Gatsby off a speeding ticket when he is shown the Police Commissioner's Christmas card to Gatsby
- State Senator Gulick's 'association' with Newton Orchid, who controls Films Par Excellence

The depressed
- the red-haired chorus girl who sings and cries and collapses at one of Gatsby's parties (52)

The suicidal
- Henry L. Palmetto who jumps in front of a subway train in Times Square; George Wilson

Adulterers
- the three Mr Mumbles with their girlfriends (45)
- Mrs Claud Roosevelt's dalliance with Owl Eyes (she left him in Gatsby's library)
- Hubert Auerbach and Mr Chrystie's wife

Deviants
- Benny McClenahan, who always arrives at Gatsby's parties with four girls
- Wolfshiem, the man with the molar cufflinks

The maimed

- the Buchanans' butler, young Brewer, who had his nose shot off in the war

Cheats

- Jordan Baker, who cheats at golf and lies about leaving a borrowed car out in the rain with the top down
- Myrtle Wilson, who cheats on her husband
- Daisy Buchanan, who cheats on her husband and evades her responsibility for Myrtle's death
- Tom Buchanan, in his many sprees and in his intimation to George Wilson that it was Gatsby who had run down his wife

Bullies

- Tom Buchanan

Arguments

- Gatsby's party (Chapter III) is disrupted by the universal arguments—even amongst the East Egg party of Jordan Baker's (52)
- the wife who interrupts her husband's conversation with a young actress and is carried off for her trouble (53)
- the director and the starlet at the second big party of Gatsby's attended by the Buchanans
- the argument between Tom and Gatsby over Daisy in the Plaza Hotel suite
- Clarence Endive's fight with Etty

Accidents

- the motor vehicle accidents of Daisy, Gatsby, Owl Eyes and Mrs Ulysses Swett
- the drowning of Dr Webster Civet

Murders

- the deaths of Gatsby and Myrtle
- Muldoon, who strangled his wife
- the suspicious circumstances surrounding the death of Dan Cody
- the gangland execution of Rosy Rosenthal.

9. 'The Great Gatsby is a novel of complex narrative structure'. Discuss.
This question is a demanding one: it requires an understanding of the jigsaw of experiences in the novel that collectively define the enigma that is Gatsby. Its focal point is Fitzgerald's device of a first-person narrator.

Checklist

- Nick is the intelligent and sympathetic observer whose ability to attract the confidences of others and whose honesty in reporting give a sense of

intensity and veracity to his narrative; he brings his Middle Western moral judgment to his experiences in the East; his appreciation of beauty gives a lyrical quality to much of his reportage.

- Nick has his own story—as he tells the story of Gatsby and the experiences he enjoyed as a result of his acquaintance with the man, Nick undertakes his own journey from innocence to experience and from the grotesqueries of Long Island back to the sanities of the Middle West.
- Nick is at the centre of things, tied into the story by many threads: he is a distant relative of Daisy Buchanan; Tom is an old but distant acquaintance from Yale; Gatsby is his neighbour; and Jordan Baker becomes his girlfriend. With these connections, Nick is able to get into the heart of things.
- Nick's own affair with Jordan Baker parallels Gatsby's affair five years before with Daisy Fay, with one important difference. Nick identifies the fickleness and dishonesty in Jordan's character and resists the temptation to be obsessed with her.
- Most of the novel is Nick's eyewitness account of events. He is present not only at Gatsby's parties, but also in Tom's house; at Myrtle's apartment; at Gatsby's reunion with Daisy (which he actually organises); at her tour of his house; at the Plaza Hotel suite when Gatsby is defeated by Tom and his dream destroyed; at Gatsby's home just after his death; at Gatsby's funeral.
- Other parts of the story are derived from other people's accounts of events, which Nick sometimes presents verbatim. Examples are Jordan Baker's account of the wartime romance between Gatsby and Daisy, which Nick reports as Jordan's eyewitness account; and Gatsby's own account of his time with Dan Cody, which Nick reports in Gatby's words, adding his own speculation.
- Occasionally, Nick reconstructs events from various sources—newspapers, servants and, as a last resort, his own imagination. These fragments he blends into his own version of events—an especially important technique in tracing George Wilson's last steps to Gatsby's house and in the actual details of Gatsby's murder.
- Nick presents three different versions of the love affair between Daisy and Gatsby (Chapters IV, VI and VII), each from a different point of view—the event is after all, the foundation of Gatsby's giant romantic illusion.
- The mixture of point of view contributes much to the realism and sense of authenticity of the narrative.
- Nick's narrative of events has an extra symbolic framework in the set pieces: Gatsby on his front steps; Tom Buchanan at his front door; Daisy and Tom sitting in their kitchen in silent conspiracy and mutual support; Gatsby standing outside the Buchanan house, watching over nothing; Gatsby in his pink suit saying his last farewell to Nick; the body floating on the pool.